THE
WORKS
OF

MENCIUS

TRANSLATOR

JAMES LEGGE

British Library Cataloguing in Publication Data

A catalogue record for this book is available from the British Library

ISBN-13: 978-1-913751-11-1

Cover Illustration:
Seated Mencius. Artist unknown

CONTENTS

CHAPTER 1

1. Mencius went to see king Hûi of Liang.

2. The king said, 'Venerable sir, since you have not counted it far to come here, a distance of a thousand lî, may I presume that you are provided with counsels to profit my kingdom?'

3. Mencius replied, 'Why must your Majesty use that word "profit?" What I am provided with, are counsels to benevolence and righteousness, and these are my only topics.

4. 'If your Majesty say, "What is to be done to profit my kingdom?" the great officers will say, "What is to be done to profit our families?" and the inferior officers and the common people will say, "What is to be done to profit our persons?" Superiors and inferiors will try to snatch this profit the one from the other, and the kingdom will be endangered. In the kingdom of ten thousand chariots, the murderer of his sovereign shall be the chief of a family of a thousand chariots. In the kingdom of a thousand chariots, the murderer of his prince shall be the chief of a family of a hundred chariots. To have a thousand in ten thousand, and a hundred in a thousand, cannot be said not to be a large allotment, but if righteousness be put last, and profit be put first, they will not be satisfied without snatching all.

5. 'There never has been a benevolent man who neglected his parents. There never has been a righteous man who made his sovereign an after consideration.

6. 'Let your Majesty also say, "Benevolence and righteousness, and let these be your only themes." Why must you use that word – "profit?".

•

1. Mencius, another day, saw King Hûi of Liang. The king went and stood with him by a pond, and, looking round at the large geese and deer, said, 'Do wise and good princes also find pleasure in these things?'

2. Mencius replied, 'Being wise and good, they have pleasure in these things. If they are not wise and good, though they have these things, they do not find pleasure.

3. 'It is said in the Book of Poetry:

> *He measured out and commenced his marvellous tower;*
> *He measured it out and planned it.*
> *The people addressed themselves to it,*
> *And in less than a day completed it.*

When he measured and began it, he said to them –
Be not so earnest:
But the multitudes came as if they had been his children.
The king was in his marvellous park;
The does reposed about,
The does so sleek and fat:
And the white birds came glistening.
The king was by his marvellous pond;
How full was it of fishes leaping about!

'King Wan used the strength of the people to make his tower and his pond, and yet the people rejoiced to do the work, calling the tower "the marvellous tower," calling the pond "the marvellous pond," and rejoicing that he had his large deer, his fishes, and turtles. The ancients caused the people to have pleasure as well as themselves, and therefore they could enjoy it.

4. 'In the Declaration of T'ang it is said, "O sun, when wilt thou expire? We will die together with thee." The people wished for Chieh's death, though they should die with him. Although he had towers, ponds, birds, and animals, how could he have pleasure alone?'

•

1. King Hûi of Liang said, 'Small as my virtue is, in the government of my kingdom, I do indeed exert my mind to the utmost. If the year be bad on the inside of the river, I remove as many of the people as I can to the east of the river, and convey grain to the country in the inside. When the year is bad on the east of the river, I act on the same plan. On examining the government of the neighboring kingdoms, I do not find that there is any prince who exerts his mind as I do. And yet the people of the neighboring kingdoms do not decrease, nor do my people increase. How is this?'

2. Mencius replied, 'Your majesty is fond of war; – let me take an illustration from war. – The soldiers move forward to the sound of the drums; and after their weapons have been crossed, on one side they throw away their coats of mail, trail their arms behind them, and run. Some run a hundred paces and stop; some run fifty paces and stop. What would you think if those who run fifty paces were to laugh at those who run a hundred paces?' The kind said, 'They should not do so. Though they did not run a hundred paces, yet they also ran away.' 'Since your Majesty knows this,' replied Mencius, 'you need not hope that your people will become more numerous than those of the neighboring kingdoms.

3. 'If the seasons of husbandry be not interfered with, the grain will be more than can be eaten. If close nets are not allowed to enter the pools and ponds, the fishes and turtles will be more than can be consumed. If the axes and bills enter

the hills and forests only at the proper time, the wood will be more than can be used. When the grain and fish and turtles are more than can be eaten, and there is more wood than can be used, this enables the people to nourish their living and mourn for their dead, without any feeling against any. This condition, in which the people nourish their living and bury their dead without any feeling against any, is the first step of royal government.

4. 'Let mulberry trees be planted about the homesteads with their five mâu, and persons of fifty years may be clothed with silk. In keeping fowls, pigs, dogs, and swine, let not their times of breeding be neglected, and persons of seventy years may eat flesh. Let there not be taken away the time that is proper for the cultivation of the farm with its hundred mâ, and the family of several mouths that is supported by it shall not suffer from hunger. Let careful attention be paid to education in schools, inculcating in it especially the filial and fraternal duties, and grey-haired men will not be seen upon the roads, carrying burdens on their backs or on their heads. It never has been that the ruler of a State, where such results were seen, – persons of seventy wearing silk and eating flesh, and the black-haired people suffering neither from hunger nor cold, – did not attain to the royal dignity.

5. 'Your dogs and swine eat the food of men, and you do not make any restrictive arrangements. There are people dying from famine on the roads, and you do not issue the stores of your granaries for them. When people die, you say, "It is not owing to me; it is owing to the year." In what does this differ from stabbing a man and killing him, and then saying – "It was not I; it was the weapon?" Let your Majesty cease to lay the blame on the year, and instantly from all the nation the people will come to you.'

•

1. King Hûi of Liang said, 'I wish quietly to receive your instructions.'

2. Mencius replied, 'Is there any difference between killing a man with a stick and with a sword ?' The king said, 'There is no difference!

3. 'Is there any difference between doing it with a sword and with the style of government? 'There is no difference,' was the reply.

4. Mencius then said, 'In your kitchen there is fat meat; in your stables there are fat horses. But your people have the look of hunger, and on the wilds there are those who have died of famine. This is leading on beasts to devour men.

5. 'Beasts devour one another, and men hate them for doing so. When a prince, being the parent of his people, administers his government so as to be chargeable with leading on beasts to devour men, where is his parental relation to the people?'

6. Chung-nî said, 'Was he not without posterity who first made wooden

images to bury with the dead? So he said, because that man made the semblances of men, and used them for that purpose:– what shall be thought of him who causes his people to die of hunger?'

•

1. King Hûi of Liang said, 'There was not in the nation a stronger State than Tsin, as you, venerable Sir, know. But since it descended to me, on the east we have been defeated by Ch'i, and then my eldest son perished; on the west we have lost seven hundred lî of territory to Ch'in; and on the south we have sustained disgrace at the hands of Ch'û. I have brought shame on my departed predecessors, and wish on their account to wipe it away, once for all. What course is to be pursued to accomplish this?'

2. Mencius replied, 'With a territory which is only a hundred lî square, it is possible to attain to the royal dignity.

3. 'If Your Majesty will indeed dispense a benevolent government to the people, being sparing in the use of punishments and fines, and making the taxes and levies light, so causing that the fields shall be ploughed deep, and the weeding of them be carefully attended to, and that the strong-bodied, during their days of leisure, shall cultivate their filial piety, fraternal respectfulness, sincerity, and truthfulness, serving thereby, at home, their fathers and elder brothers, and, abroad, their elders and superiors.– you will then have a people who can be employed, with sticks which they have prepared, to oppose the strong mail and sharp weapons of the troops of Ch'in and Ch'û.

4. 'The rulers of those States rob their people of their time, so that they cannot plough and weed their fields, in order to support their parents. Their parents suffer from cold and hunger. Brothers, wives, and children are separated and scattered abroad.

5. 'Those rulers, as it were, drive their people into pit-falls, or drown them. Your Majesty will go to punish them. In such a case, who will oppose your Majesty?

6. 'In accordance with this is the saying,– "The benevolent has no enemy." I beg your Majesty not to doubt what I say.'

CHAPTER 2

1. Mencius went to see the king Hsiang of Liang.

2. On coming out from the interview, he said to some persons, 'When I looked at him from a distance, he did not appear like a sovereign; when I drew near to him, I saw nothing venerable about him. Abruptly he asked me, "How can the kingdom be settled?" I replied, "It will be settled by being united under one sway."

3. '"Who can so unite it?"

4. 'I replied, "He who has no pleasure in killing men can so unite it."

5. '"Who can give it to him?"

6. 'I replied, " All the people of the nation will unanimously give it to him. Does your Majesty understand the way of the growing grain? During the seventh and eighth months, when drought prevails, the plants become dry. Then the clouds collect densely in the heavens, they send down torrents of rain, and the grain erects itself, as if by a shoot. When it does so, who can keep it back? Now among the shepherds of men throughout the nation, there is not one who does not find pleasure in killing men. If there were one who did not find pleasure in killing men, all the people in the nation would look towards him with outstretched necks. Such being indeed the case, the people would flock to him, as water flows downwards with a rush, which no one can repress."'

•

1. The king Hsüan of Ch'î asked, saying, 'May I be informed by you of the transactions of Hwan of Ch'î, and Wan of Tsin?'

2. Mencius replied, 'There were none of the disciples of Chung-nî who spoke about the affairs of Hwan and Wan, and therefore they have not been transmitted to these after-ages ;– your servant has not heard them. If you will have me speak, let it be about royal government.'

3. The king said, 'What virtue must there be in order to attain to royal sway?' Mencius answered, 'The love and protection of the people; with this there is no power which can prevent a ruler from attaining to it.'

4. The king asked again, 'Is such an one as I competent to love and protect the people?' Mencius said, 'Yes.' 'How do you know that I am competent for that?' 'I heard the following incident from Hû Ho:– "The king," said he, "was sitting aloft in the hall, when a man appeared, leading an ox past the lower part

8

of it. The king saw him, and asked, Where is the ox going? The man replied, We are going to consecrate a bell with its blood. The king said, Let it go. I cannot bear its frightened appearance, as if it were an innocent person going to the place of death. The man answered, Shall we then omit the consecration of the bell ? The king said, How can that be omitted? Change it for a sheep." I do not know whether this incident really occurred.'

5. The king replied, 'It did,' and then Mencius said, 'The heart seen in this is sufficient to carry you to the royal sway. The people all supposed that your Majesty grudged the animal, but your servant knows surely, that it was your Majesty's not being able to bear the sight, which made you do as you did.'

6. The king said, 'You are right. And yet there really was an appearance of what the people condemned. But though Chî be a small and narrow State, how should I grudge one ox? Indeed it was because I could not bear its frightened appearance, as if it were an innocent person going to the place of death, that therefore I changed it for a sheep.'

7. Mencius pursued, 'Let not your Majesty deem it strange that the people should think you were grudging the animal. When you changed a large one for a small, how should they know the true reason? If you felt pained by its being led without guilt to the place of death, what was there to choose between an ox and a sheep? The king laughed and said, 'What really was my mind in the matter? I did not grudge the expense of it, and changed it for a sheep!– There was reason in the people's saying that I grudged it.'

8. 'There is no harm in their saying so,' said Mencius. 'Your conduct was an artifice of benevolence. You saw the ox, and had not seen the sheep. So is the superior man affected towards animals, that, having seen them alive, he cannot bear to see them die; having heard their dying cries, he cannot bear to eat their flesh. Therefore he keeps away from his slaughter-house and cook-room.'

9. The king was pleased, and said, 'It is said in the Book of Poetry, "The minds of others, I am able by reflection to measure;" – this is verified, my Master, in your discovery of my motive. I indeed did the thing, but when I turned my thoughts inward, and examined into it, I could not discover my own mind. When you, Master, spoke those words, the movements of compassion began to work in my mind. How is it that this heart has in it what is equal to the royal sway?'

10. Mencius replied, 'Suppose a man were to make this statement to your Majesty:– "My strength is sufficient to lift three thousand catties, but it is not sufficient to lift one feather;– my eyesight is sharp enough to examine the point of an autumn hair, but I do not see a waggon-load of faggots;– "would your Majesty allow what he said?' 'No,' was the answer, on which Mencius

proceeded, 'Now here is kindness sufficient to reach to animals, and no benefits are extended from it to the people.– How is this? Is an exception to be made here? The truth is, the feather is not lifted , because strength is not used; the waggon-load of firewood is not seen, because the eyesight is not used; and the people are not loved and protected, because kindness is not employed. Therefore your Majesty's not exercising the royal sway, is because you do not do it, not because you are not able to do it.'

11. The king asked, 'How may the difference between the not doing a thing, and the not being able to do it, be represented? Mencius replied,'In such a thing as taking the T'âi mountain under your arm, and leaping over the north sea with it, if you say to people– "I am not able to do it," that is a real case of not being able. In such a matter as breaking off a branch from a tree at the order of a superior, if you say to people– "I am not able to do it," that is a case of not doing it, it is not a case of not being able to do it. Therefore your Majesty's not exercising the royal sway, is not such a case as that of taking the T'âi mountain under your arm, and leaping over the north sea with it. Your Majesty's not exercising the royal sway is a case like that of breaking off a branch from a tree.

12. 'Treat with the reverence due to age the elders in your own family, so that the elders in the families of others shall be similarly treated; treat with the kindness due to youth the young in your own family, so that the young in the families of others shall be similarly treated:– do this, and the kingdom may be made to go round in your palm. It is said in the Book of Poetry, "His example affected his wife. It reached to his brothers, and his family of the State was governed by it."– The language shows how king Wan simply took his kindly heart, and exercised it towards those parties. Therefore the carrying out his kindness of heart by a prince will suffice for the love and protection of all within the four seas, and if he do not carry it out, he will not be able to protect his wife and children. The way in which the ancients came greatly to surpass other men, was no other but this:– simply that they knew well how to carry out, so as to affect others, what they themselves did. Now your kindness is sufficient to reach to animals, and no benefits are extended from it to reach the people.– How is this? Is an exception to be made here?

13. 'By weighing, we know what things are light, and what heavy. By measuring, we know what things are long, and what short. The relations of all things may be thus determined, and it is of the greatest importance to estimate the motions of the mind. I beg your Majesty to measure it.

14. 'You collect your equipments of war, endanger your soldiers and officers, and excite the resentment of the other princes;– do these things cause you pleasure in your mind?'

15. The king replied, 'No. How should I derive pleasure from these things? My object in them is to seek for what I greatly desire.'

16. Mencius said, 'May I hear from you what it is that you greatly desire?' The king laughed and did not speak. Mencius resumed, 'Are you led to desire it, because you have not enough of rich and sweet food for your mouth? Or because you have not enough of light and warm clothing for your body? Or because you have not enough of beautifully coloured objects to delight your eyes? Or because you have not voices and tones enough to please your ears? Or because you have not enough of attendants and favourites to stand before you and receive your orders? Your Majesty's various officers are sufficient to supply you with those things. How can your Majesty be led to entertain such a desire on account of them?' 'No,' said the king; 'my desire is not on account of them.' Mencius added, 'Then, what your Majesty greatly desires may be known. You wish to enlarge your territories, to have Ch'in and Ch'û wait at your court, to rule the Middle Kingdom, and to attract to you the barbarous tribes that surround it. But doing what you do to seek for what you desire is like climbing a tree to seek for fish.'

17. The king said, 'Is it so bad as that?' 'It is even worse,' was the reply. 'If you climb a tree to seek for fish, although you do not get the fish, you will not suffer any subsequent calamity. But doing what you do, to seek for what you desire, doing it moreover with all your heart, you will assuredly afterwards meet with calamities.' The king asked, 'May I hear from you the proof of that?' Mencius said, 'If the people of Tsâu should fight with the people of Ch'û, which of them does your Majesty think would conquer?' 'The people of Ch'û would conquer.' 'Yes;– and so it is certain that a small country cannot contend with a great, that few cannot contend with many, that the weak cannot contend with the strong. The territory within the four seas embraces nine divisions, each of a thousand lî square. All Ch'î together is but one of them. If with one part you try to subdue the other eight, what is the difference between that and Tsâu's contending with Ch'û? For, with such a desire, you must turn back to the proper course for its attainment.

18. 'Now if your Majesty will institute a government whose action shall be benevolent, this will cause all the officers in the kingdom to wish to stand in your Majesty's court, and all the farmers to wish to plough in your Majesty's fields, and all the merchants, both travelling and stationary, to wish to store their goods in your Majesty's market-places, and all travelling strangers to wish to make their tours on your Majesty's roads, and all throughout the kingdom who feel aggrieved by their rulers to wish to come and complain to your Majesty. And when they are so bent, who will be able to keep them back?'

19. The king said, 'I am stupid, and not able to advance to this. I wish you, my Master, to assist my intentions. Teach me clearly; although I am deficient in intelligence and vigour, I will essay and try to carry your instructions into effect.'

20. Mencius replied, 'They are only men of education, who, without a certain livelihood, are able to maintain a fixed heart. As to the people, if they have not a certain livelihood, it follows that they will not have a fixed heart. And if they have not a fixed heart, there is nothing which they will not do, in the way of self-abandonment, of moral deflection, of depravity, and of wild license. When they thus have been involved in crime, to follow them up and punish them;– this is to entrap the people. How can such a thing as entrapping the people be done under the rule of a benevolent man?

21. 'Therefore an intelligent ruler will regulate the livelihood of the people, so as to make sure that, for those above them, they shall have sufficient wherewith to serve their parents, and, for those below them, sufficient wherewith to support their wives and children; that in good years they shall always be abundantly satisfied, and that in bad years they shall escape the danger of perishing. After this he may urge them, and they will proceed to what is good, for in this case the people will follow after it with ease.

22. 'Now, the livelihood of the people is so regulated, that, above, they have not sufficient wherewith to serve their parents, and, below, they have not sufficient wherewith to support their wives and children. Notwithstanding good years, their lives are continually embittered, and, in bad years, they do not escape perishing. In such circumstances they only try to save themselves from death, and are afraid they will not succeed. What leisure have they to cultivate propriety and righteousness?'

23. 'If your Majesty wishes to effect this regulation of the livelihood of the people, why not turn to that which is the essential step to it?

24. 'Let mulberry-trees be planted about the homesteads with their five mâu, and persons of fifty years may be clothed with silk. In keeping fowls, pigs, dogs, and swine, let not their times of breeding be neglected, and persons of seventy years may eat flesh. Let there not be taken away the time that is proper for the cultivation of the farm with its hundred mâu, and the family of eight mouths that is supported by it shall not suffer from hunger. Let careful attention be paid to education in schools,– the inculcation in it especially of the filial and fraternal duties, and grey-haired men will not be seen upon the roads, carrying burdens on their backs or on their heads. It never has been that the ruler of a State where such results were seen,– the old wearing silk and eating flesh, and the black-haired people suffering neither from hunger nor cold,– did not attain to the royal dignity.'

CHAPTER 3

1. Chwang Pâ'o, seeing Mencius, said to him, 'I had an interview with the king. His Majesty told me that he loved music, and I was not prepared with anything to reply to him. What do you pronounce about that love of music?' Mencius replied, 'If the king's love of music were very great, the kingdom of Ch'î would be near to a state of good government!'

2. Another day, Mencius, having an interview with the king, said, 'Your Majesty, I have heard, told the officer Chwang, that you love music;– was it so?' The king changed colour, and said, 'I am unable to love the music of the ancient sovereigns; I only love the music that suits the manners of the present age.'

3. Mencius said, 'If your Majesty's love of music were very great, Ch'î would be near to a state of good government! The music of the present day is just like the music of antiquity, as regards effecting that.'

4. The king said, 'May I hear from you the proof of that?' Mencius asked, 'Which is the more pleasant,– to enjoy music by yourself alone, or to enjoy it with others?' 'To enjoy it with others,' was the reply. 'And which is the more pleasant,– to enjoy music with a few, or to enjoy it with many?' 'To enjoy it with many.'

5. Mencius proceeded, 'Your servant begs to explain what I have said about music to your Majesty.

6. 'Now, your Majesty is having music here.– The people hear the noise of your bells and drums, and the notes of your fifes and pipes, and they all, with aching heads, knit their brows, and say to one another, "That's how our king likes his music! But why does he reduce us to this extremity of distress?– Fathers and sons cannot see one another. Elder brothers and younger brothers, wives and children, are separated and scattered abroad." Now, your Majesty is hunting here.– The people hear the noise of your carriages and horses, and see the beauty of your plumes and streamers, and they all, with aching heads, knit their brows, and say to one another, "That's how our king likes his hunting! But why does he reduce us to this extremity of distress?– Fathers and sons cannot see one another. Elder brothers and younger brothers, wives and children, are separated and scattered abroad." Their feeling thus is from no other reason but that you do not allow the people to have pleasure as well as yourself.

7. 'Now, your Majesty is having music here. The people hear the noise of your bells and drums, and the notes of your fifes and pipes, and they all, delighted, and

with joyful looks, say to one another, "That sounds as if our king were free from all sickness! If he were not, how could he enjoy this music?" Now, your Majesty is hunting here.– The people hear the noise of your carriages and horses, and see the beauty of your plumes and streamers, and they all, delighted, and with joyful looks, say to one another, "That looks as if our king were free from all sickness! If he were not, how could he enjoy this hunting?" Their feeling thus is from no other reason but that you cause them to have their pleasure as you have yours.

8. 'If your Majesty now will make pleasure a thing common to the people and yourself, the royal sway awaits you.'

●

1. The king Hsüan of Ch'î asked, 'Was it so, that the park of king Wan contained seventy square lî?' Mencius replied, 'It is so in the records.'

2. 'Was it so large as that?' exclaimed the king. 'The people,' said Mencius, 'still looked on it as small.' The king added, 'My park contains only forty square lî, and the people still look on it as large. How is this?' 'The park of king Wan,' was the reply, 'contained seventy square lî, but the grass-cutters and fuel-gatherers had the privilege of entrance into it; so also had the catchers of pheasants and hares. He shared it with the people, and was it not with reason that they looked on it as small?

3. 'When I first arrived at the borders of your kingdom, I inquired about the great prohibitory regulations, before I would venture to enter it; and I heard, that inside the barrier-gates there was a park of forty square lî, and that he who killed a deer in it, was held guilty of the same crime as if he had killed a man.– Thus those forty square lî are a pitfall in the middle of the kingdom. Is it not with reason that the people look upon them as large?'

●

1. The king Hsüan of Ch'î asked, saying, 'Is there any way to regulate one's maintenance of intercourse with neighbouring kingdoms?' Mencius replied, 'There is. But it requires a perfectly virtuous prince to be able, with a great country, to serve a small one,– as, for instance, T'ang served Ko, and king Wan served the Kwan barbarians. And it requires a wise prince to be able, with a small country, to serve a large one,– as the king T'âi served the Hsün-yü, and Kâu-ch'ien served Wû.

2. 'He who with a great State serves a small one, delights in Heaven. He who with a small State serves a large one, stands in awe of Heaven. He who delights in Heaven, will affect with his love and protection the whole kingdom. He who stands in awe of Heaven, will affect with his love and protection his own kingdom.

3. 'It is said in the Book of Poetry, "I fear the Majesty of Heaven, and will thus preserve its favouring decree."'

4. The king said, 'Agreat saying! But I have an infirmity;– I love valour.'

5. 'I beg your Majesty,' was the reply, 'not to love small valour. If a man brandishes his sword, looks fiercely, and says, "How dare he withstand me?"– this is the valour of a common man, who can be the opponent only of a single individual. I beg your Majesty to greaten it.

6. 'It is said in the *Book of Poetry*:

The king blazed with anger,
And he marshalled his hosts,
To stop the march to Chü,
To consolidate the prosperity of Châu,
To meet the expectations of the nation.

This was the valour of king Wan. King Wan, in one burst of his anger, gave repose to all the people of the kingdom.

7. 'In the Book of History it is said, "Heaven having produced the inferior people, made for them rulers and teachers, with the purpose that they should be assisting to God, and therefore distinguished them throughout the four quarters of the land. Whoever are offenders, and whoever are innocent, here am I to deal with them. How dare any under heaven give indulgence to their refractory wills?" There was one man pursuing a violent and disorderly course in the kingdom, and king Wû was ashamed of it. This was the valour of king Wû. He also, by one display of his anger, gave repose to all the people of the kingdom.

8. 'Let now your Majesty also, in one burst of anger, give repose to all the people of the kingdom. The people are only afraid that your Majesty does not love valour.'

•

1. The king Hsüan of Ch'î had an interview with Mencius in the Snow palace, and said to him, 'Do men of talents and worth likewise find pleasure in these things?' Mencius replied, 'They do; and if people generally are not able to enjoy themselves, they condemn their superiors.

2. 'For them, when they cannot enjoy themselves, to condemn their superiors is wrong, but when the superiors of the people do not make enjoyment a thing common to the people and themselves, they also do wrong.

3. 'When a ruler rejoices in the joy of his people, they also rejoice in his joy; when he grieves at the sorrow of his people, they also grieve at his sorrow. A sympathy of joy will pervade the kingdom ; a sympathy of sorrow will do the

same:– in such a state of things, it cannot be but that the ruler attain to the royal dignity.

4. 'Formerly, the duke Ching of Ch'î asked the minister Yen, saying, "I wish to pay a visit of inspection to Chuan-fû, and Châo-wû, and then to bend my course southward along the shore, till I come to Lang-yê. What shall I do that my tour may be fit to be compared with the visits of inspection made by the ancient sovereigns?"

5. 'The minister Yen replied, "An excellent inquiry! When the Son of Heaven visited the princes, it was called a tour of inspection, that is, he surveyed the States under their care. When the princes attended at the court of the Son of Heaven, it was called a report of office, that is, they reported their administration of their offices. Thus, neither of the proceedings was without a purpose. And moreover, in the spring they examined the ploughing, and supplied any deficiency of seed; in the autumn they examined the reaping, and supplied any deficiency of yield. There is the saying of the Hsiâ dynasty,– If our king do not take his ramble, what will become of our happiness? If our king do not make his excursion, what will become of our help? That ramble, and that excursion, were a pattern to the princes.

6. '"Now, the state of things is different.– A host marches in attendance on the ruler, and stores of provisions are consumed. The hungry are deprived of their food, and there is no rest for those who are called to toil. Maledictions are uttered by one to another with eyes askance, and the people proceed to the commission of wickedness. Thus the royal ordinances are violated, and the people are oppressed, and the supplies of food and drink flow away like water. The rulers yield themselves to the current, or they urge their way against it; they are wild; they are utterly lost:– these things proceed to the grief of the inferior princes.

7. '"Descending along with the current, and forgetting to return, is what I call yielding to it. Pressing up against it, and forgetting to return, is what I call urging their way against it. Pursuing the chase without satiety is what I call being wild. Delighting in wine without satiety is what I call being lost.

8. '"The ancient sovereigns had no pleasures to which they gave themselves as on the flowing stream; no doings which might be so characterized as wild and lost.

9. '"It is for you, my prince, to pursue your course."'

10. 'The duke Ching was pleased. He issued a proclamation throughout his State, and went out and occupied a shed in the borders. From that time he began to open his granaries to supply the wants of the people, and calling

the Grand music-master, he said to him– "Make for me music to suit a prince and his minister pleased with each other." And it was then that the Chî-shâo and Chio-shâo were made, in the words to which it was said, "Is it a fault to restrain one's prince?" He who restrains his prince loves his prince.'

•

1. The king Hsüan of Ch'î said, 'People all tell me to pull down and remove the Hall of Distinction. Shall I pull it down, or stop the movement for that object?'

2. Mencius replied, 'The Hall of Distinction is a Hall appropriate to the sovereigns. If your Majesty wishes to practise the true royal government, then do not pull it down.'

3. The king said, 'May I hear from you what the true royal government is?' 'Formerly,' was the reply, 'king Wan's government of Ch'î was as follows:– The husbandmen cultivated for the government one-ninth of the land; the descendants of officers were salaried; at the passes and in the markets, strangers were inspected, but goods were not taxed: there were no prohibitions respecting the ponds and weirs; the wives and children of criminals were not involved in their guilt. There were the old and wifeless, or widowers; the old and husbandless, or widows; the old and childless, or solitaries ; the young and fatherless, or orphans:– these four classes are the most destitute of the people, and have none to whom they can tell their wants, and king Wan, in the institution of his government with its benevolent action, made them the first objects of his regard, as it is said in the *Book of Poetry*:

> *The rich may get through life well;*
> *But alas! for the miserable and solitary!*

4. The king said, 'O excellent words!' Mencius said, 'Since your Majesty deems them excellent, why do you not practise them?' 'I have an infirmity,' said the king; 'I am fond of wealth.' The reply was, 'Formerly, Kung-lîu was fond of wealth. It is said in the Book of Poetry:

> *He reared his ricks, and filled his granaries,*
> *He tied up dried provisions and grain,*
> *In bottomless bags, and sacks,*
> *That he might gather his people together, and glorify his State.*
> *With bows and arrows all displayed,*
> *With shields, and spears, and battle-axes, large and small,*
> *He commenced his march.*

In this way those who remained in their old seat had their ricks and granaries, and those who marched had their bags of provisions. It was not till after this that he thought he could begin his march. If your Majesty loves wealth, give the people power to gratify the same feeling, and what difficulty will there be in your attaining the royal sway?'

5. The king said, 'I have an infirmity; I am fond of beauty.' The reply was, 'Formerly, king T'âi was fond of beauty, and loved his wife. It is said in the Book of Poetry:

> *Kû-kung T'an-fû*
> *Came in the morning, galloping his horse,*
> *By the banks of the western waters,*
> *As far as the foot of Ch'î hill,*
> *Along with the lady of Chiang;*
> *They came and together chose the site for their settlement.*

At that time, in the seclusion of the house, there were no dissatisfied women, and abroad, there were no unmarried men. If your Majesty loves beauty, let the people be able to gratify the same feeling, and what difficulty will there be in your attaining the royal sway?'

•

1. Mencius said to the king Hsüan of Ch'î, 'Suppose that one of your Majesty's ministers were to entrust his wife and children to the care of his friend, while he himself went into Ch'û to travel, and that, on his return, he should find that the friend had let his wife and children suffer from cold and hunger;– how ought he to deal with him?' The king said, 'He should cast him off.'

2. Mencius proceeded, 'Suppose that the chief criminal judge could not regulate the officers under him, how would you deal with him?' The king said, 'Dismiss him.'

3. Mencius again said, 'If within the four borders of your kingdom there is not good government, what is to be done?' The king looked to the right and left, and spoke of other matters.

CHAPTER 4

1. Mencius, having an interview with the king Hsüan of Ch'î, said to him, 'When men speak of "an ancient kingdom," it is not meant thereby that it has lofty trees in it, but that it has ministers sprung from families which have been noted in it for generations. Your Majesty has no intimate ministers even. Those whom you advanced yesterday are gone to-day, and you do not know it.'

2. The king said, 'How shall I know that they have not ability, and so avoid employing them at all?'

3. The reply was, 'The ruler of a State advances to office men of talents and virtue only as a matter of necessity. Since he will thereby cause the low to overstep the honourable, and distant to overstep his near relatives, ought he to do so but with caution?

4. 'When all those about you say,– "This is a man of talents and worth," you may not therefore believe it. When your great officers all say,– "This is a man of talents and virtue," neither may you for that believe it. When all the people say,– "This is a man of talents and virtue," then examine into the case, and when you find that the man is such, employ him. When all those about you say,– "This man won't do," don't listen to them. When all your great officers say,– "This man won't do," don't listen to them. When the people all say,– "This man won't do," then examine into the case, and when you find that the man won't do, send him away.

5. 'When all those about you say,– "This man deserves death," don't listen to them. When all your great officers say,– "This man deserves death," don't listen to them. When the people all say,"This man deserves death," then inquire into the case, and when you see that the man deserves death, put him to death. In accordance with this we have the saying, "The people killed him."

6. 'You must act in this way in order to be the parent of the people.'

•

1. The king Hsüan of Ch'î asked, saying, 'Was it so, that T'ang banished Chieh, and that king Wû smote Châu?' Mencius replied, 'It is so in the records.'

2. The king said, 'May a minister then put his sovereign to death?'

3. Mencius said, 'He who outrages the benevolence proper to his nature, is called a robber; he who outrages righteousness, is called a ruffian. The robber and ruffian we call a mere fellow. I have heard of the cutting off of the fellow Châu, but I have not heard of the putting a sovereign to death, in his case.'

•

1. Mencius, having an interview with the king Hsüan of Ch'î, said to him, 'If you are going to build a large mansion, you will surely cause the Master of the workmen to look out for large trees, and when he has found such large trees, you will be glad, thinking that they will answer for the intended object. Should the workmen hew them so as to make them too small, then your Majesty will be angry, thinking that they will not answer for the purpose. Now, a man spends his youth in learning the principles of right government, and, being grown up to vigour, he wishes to put them in practice;– if your Majesty says to him, "For the present put aside what you have learned, and follow me," what shall we say?

2. 'Here now you have a gem unwrought, in the stone. Although it may be worth 240,000 taels, you will surely employ a lapidary to cut and polish it. But when you come to the government of the State, then you say,– "For the present put aside what you have learned, and follow me." How is it that you herein act so differently from your conduct in calling in the lapidary to cut the gem?'

•

1. The people of Ch'î attacked Yen, and conquered it.

2. The king Hsüan asked, saying, 'Some tell me not to take possession of it for myself, and some tell me to take possession of it. For a kingdom of ten thousand chariots, attacking another of ten thousand chariots, to complete the conquest of it in fifty days, is an achievement beyond mere human strength. If I do not take possession of it, calamities from Heaven will surely come upon me. What do you say to my taking possession of it?'

3. Mencius replied, 'If the people of Yen will be pleased with your taking possession of it, then do so.– Among the ancients there was one who acted on this principle, namely king Wû. If the people of Yen will not be pleased with your taking possession of it, then do not do so.– Among the ancients there was one who acted on this principle, namely king Wan.

4. 'When, with all the strength of your country of ten thousand chariots, you attacked another country of ten thousand chariots, and the people brought baskets of rice and vessels of congee, to meet your Majesty's host, was there any other reason for this but that they hoped to escape out of fire and water ? If you make the water more deep and the fire more fierce, they will in like manner make another revolution.'

•

1. The people of Ch'î, having smitten Yen, took possession of it, and upon this, the princes of the various States deliberated together, and resolved to deliver Yen from their power. The king Hsüan said to Mencius, 'The princes have formed many plans to attack me:– how shall I prepare myself for them?' Mencius replied, 'I have heard of one who with seventy lî exercised all the

functions of government throughout the kingdom. That was T'ang. I have never heard of a prince with a thousand lî standing in fear of others.'

2. 'It is said in the Book of History, As soon as T'ang began his work of executing justice, he commenced with Ko. The whole kingdom had confidence in him. When he pursued his work in the east, the rude tribes on the west murmured. So did those on the north, when he was engaged in the south. Their cry was–"Why does he put us last?" Thus, the people looked to him, as we look in a time of great drought to the clouds and rainbows. The frequenters of the markets stopped not. The husbandmen made no change in their operations. While he punished their rulers, he consoled the people. His progress was like the falling of opportune rain, and the people were delighted. It is said again in the Book of History, "We have waited for our prince long; the prince's coming will be our reviving!"

3. 'Now the ruler of Yen was tyrannizing over his people, and your Majesty went and punished him. The people supposed that you were going to deliver them out of the water and the fire, and brought baskets of rice and vessels of congee, to meet your Majesty's host. But you have slain their fathers and elder brothers, and put their sons and younger brothers in confinement. You have pulled down the ancestral temple of the State, and are removing to Ch'î its precious vessels. How can this be deemed proper? The rest of the kingdom is indeed jealously afraid of the strength of Ch'î; and now, when with a doubled territory you do not put in practice a benevolent government;– it is this which sets the arms of the empire in motion.

4. 'If your Majesty will make haste to issue an ordinance, restoring your captives, old and young, stopping the removal of the precious vessels, and saying that, after consulting with the people of Yen, you will appoint them a ruler, and withdraw from the country;– in this way you may still be able to stop the threatened attack.'

•

1. There had been a brush between Tsâu and Lû, when the duke Mû asked Mencius, saying,'Of my officers there were killed thirty-three men, and none of the people would die in their defence. Though I sentenced them to death for their conduct, it is impossible to put such a multitude to death. If I do not put them to death, then there is the crime unpunished of their looking angrily on at the death of their officers, and not saving them How is the exigency of the case to be met?'

2. Mencius replied, 'In calamitous years and years of famine, the old and weak of your people, who have been found lying in the ditches and water-channels, and the able-bodied who have been scattered about to the four quarters, have amounted to several thousands. All the while, your granaries, O prince, have been stored with grain, and your treasuries and arsenals have been full, and not one of your officers has told you of the distress. Thus negligent have the superiors in your State been,

and cruel to their inferiors. The philosopher Tsang said, "Beware, beware. What proceeds from you, will return to you again." Now at length the people have paid back the conduct of their officers to them. Do not you, O prince, blame them.

3. 'If you will put in practice a benevolent government, this people will love you and all above them, and will die for their officers.'

•

1. The duke Wan of T'ang asked Mencius, saying, 'T'ang is a small kingdom, and lies between Ch'î and Ch'û. Shall I serve Ch'î? Or shall I serve Chû?'

2. Mencius replied, 'This plan which you propose is beyond me. If you will have me counsel you, there is one thing I can suggest. Dig deeper your moats; build higher your walls; guard them as well as your people. In case of attack, be prepared to die in your defence, and have the people so that they will not leave you;– this is a proper course.

•

1. The duke Wan of T'ang asked Mencius, saying, 'The people of Ch'î are going to fortify Hsieh. The movement occasions me great alarm. What is the proper course for me to take in the case?'

2. Mencius replied, 'Formerly, when king T'âi dwelt in Pin, the barbarians of the north were continually making incursions upon it. He therefore left it, went to the foot of mount Ch'î, and there took up his residence. He did not take that situation, as having selected it. It was a matter of necessity with him.

3. 'If you do good, among your descendants, in after generations, there shall be one who will attain to the royal dignity. A prince lays the foundation of the inheritance, and hands down the beginning which he has made, doing what may be continued by his successors. As to the accomplishment of the great result, that is with Heaven. What is that Ch'î to you, O prince? Be strong to do good. That is all your business.'

•

1. The duke Wan of T'ang asked Mencius, saying, 'T'ang is a small State. Though I do my utmost to serve those large kingdoms on either side of it, we cannot escape suffering from them. What course shall I take that we may do so?' Mencius replied, 'Formerly, when king T'âi dwelt in Pin, the barbarians of the north were constantly making incursions upon it. He served them with skins and silks, and still he suffered from them. He served them with dogs and horses, and still he suffered from them. He served them with pearls and gems, and still he suffered from them. Seeing this, he assembled the old men, and announced to them, saying, "What the barbarians want is my territory. I have heard this,– that a ruler does not injure his people with that wherewith he nourishes them. My children, why should you be troubled about having no prince? I will leave this." Accordingly, he left Pin,

crossed the mountain Liang, built a town at the foot of mount Ch'î, and dwelt there. The people of Pin said, "He is a benevolent man. We must not lose him." Those who followed him looked like crowds hastening to market.

2. 'On the other hand, some say, "The kingdom is a thing to be kept from generation to generation. One individual cannot undertake to dispose of it in his own person. Let him be prepared to die for it. Let him not quit it."

3. 'I ask you, prince, to make your election between these two courses.'

•

1. The duke P'ing of Lû was about to leave his palace, when his favourite, one Tsang Ts'ang, made a request to him, saying, 'On other days, when you have gone out, you have given instructions to the officers as to where you were going. But now, the horses have been put to the carriage, and the officers do not yet know where you are going. I venture to ask.' The duke said, 'I am going to see the scholar Mang.' ' How is this?' said the other. 'That you demean yourself, prince - in paying the honour of the first visit to a common man - is, I suppose, because you think that he is a man of talents and virtue. By such men the rules of ceremonial proprieties and right are observed. But on the occasion of this Mang's second mourning, his observances exceeded those of the former. Do not go to see him, my prince.' The duke said, 'I will not.'

2. The officer Yo-chang entered the court, and had an audience. He said, 'Prince, why have you not gone to see Mang K'o?' the duke said, 'One told me that, on the occasion of the scholar Mang's second mourning, his observances exceeded those of the former. It is on that account that I have not gone to see him.' 'How is this!' answered Yo-chang. 'By what you call "exceeding," you mean, I suppose, that, on the first occasion, he used the rites appropriate to a scholar, and, on the second, those appropriate to a great officer; that he first used three tripods, and afterwards five tripods.' The duke said, 'No; I refer to the greater excellence of the coffin, the shell, the grave-clothes, and the shroud.' Yo-chAng said, 'That cannot be called "exceeding." That was the difference between being poor and being rich.'

3. After this, Yo-chang saw Mencius, and said to him, 'I told the prince about you, and he was consequently coming to see you, when one of his favourites, named Tsang Ts'ang, stopped him, and therefore he did not come according to his purpose.' Mencius said, 'A man's advancement is effected, it may be, by others, and the stopping him is, it may be, from the efforts of others. But to advance a man or to stop his advance is really beyond the power of other men. My not finding in the prince of Lû a ruler who would confide in me, and put my counsels into practice, is from Heaven. How could that scion of the Tsang family cause me not to find the ruler that would suit me?'

CHAPTER 5

1. Kung-sun Ch'âu asked Mencius, saying, 'Master, if you were to obtain the ordering of the government in Ch'î, could you promise yourself to accomplish anew such results as those realized by Kwan Chung and Yen?'

2. Mencius said, 'You are indeed a true man of Ch'î. You know about Kwan Chung and Yen, and nothing more,

3. 'Some one asked Tsang Hsî, saying, "Sir, to which do you give the superiority,– to yourself or to Tsze-lû?" Tsang Hsî looked uneasy, and said, "He was an object of veneration to my grandfather." "Then," pursued the other, "Do you give the superiority to yourself or to Kwan Chung?" Tsang Hsî, flushed with anger and displeased, said, "How dare you compare me with Kwan Chung? Considering how entirely Kwan Chung possessed the confidence of his prince, how long he enjoyed the direction of the government of the State, and how low, after all, was what he accomplished,– how is it that you liken me to him?"

4. 'Thus,' concluded Mencius, 'Tsang Hsî would not play Kwan Chung, and is it what you desire for me that I should do so?'

5. Kung-sun Ch'âu said, 'Kwan Chung raised his prince to be the leader of all the other princes, and Yen made his prince illustrious, and do you still think it would not be enough for you to do what they did?'

6. Mencius answered, 'To raise Ch'î to the royal dignity would be as easy as it is to turn round the hand.'

7. 'So!' returned the other. 'The perplexity of your disciple is hereby very much increased. There was king Wan, moreover, with all the virtue which belonged to him; and who did not die till he had reached a hundred years:– and still his influence had not penetrated throughout the kingdom. It required king Wû and the duke of Châu to continue his course, before that influence greatly prevailed. Now you say that the royal dignity might be so easily obtained:– is king Wan then not a sufficient object for imitation?'

8. Mencius said, 'How can king Wan be matched? From T'ang to Wû-ting there had appeared six or seven worthy and sage sovereigns. The kingdom had been attached to Yin for a long time, and this length of time made a change difficult. Wû-ting had all the princes coming to his court, and possessed the kingdom as if it had been a thing which he moved round in his palm. Then, Châu was removed from Wû-ting by no great interval of time. There were still remaining some of the ancient families and of the old manners, of the

influence also which had emanated from the earlier sovereigns, and of their good government. Moreover, there were the viscount of Wei and his second son, their Royal Highnesses Pî-kan and the viscount of Ch'î, and Kâo-ko, all men of ability and virtue, who gave their joint assistance to Châu in his government. In consequence of these things, it took a long time for him to lose the throne. There was not a foot of ground which he did not possess. There was not one of all the people who was not his subject. So it was on his side, and king Wan at his beginning had only a territory of one hundred square lî. On all these accounts, it was difficult for him immediately to attain to the royal dignity.

9. 'The people of Ch'î have a saying– "A man may have wisdom and discernment, but that is not like embracing the favourable opportunity. A man may have instruments of husbandry, but that is not like waiting for the farming seasons." The present time is one in which the royal dignity may be easily attained.

10. 'In the flourishing periods of the Hsiâ, Yin, and Châu dynasties, the royal domain did not exceed a thousand lî, and Ch'î embraces so much territory. Cocks crow and dogs bark to one another, all the way to the four borders of the State:– so Ch'î possesses the people. No change is needed for the enlarging of its territory: no change is needed for the collecting of a population. If its ruler will put in practice a benevolent government, no power will be able to prevent his becoming sovereign.

11. 'Moreover, never was there a time farther removed than the present from the rise of a true sovereign: never was there a time when the sufferings of the people from tyrannical government were more intense than the present. The hungry readily partake of any food, and the thirsty of any drink.'

12. 'Confucius said, "The flowing progress of virtue is more rapid than the transmission of royal orders by stages and couriers."

13. 'At the present time, in a country of ten thousand chariots, let benevolent government be put in practice, and the people will be delighted with it, as if they were relieved from hanging by the heels. With half the merit of the ancients, double their achievements is sure to be realized. It is only at this time that such could be the case.'

•

1. Kung-sun Ch'âu asked Mencius, saying, 'Master, if you were to be appointed a high noble and the prime minister of Ch'î, so as to be able to carry your principles into practice, though you should thereupon raise the ruler to the headship of all the other princes, or even to the royal dignity, it would not be to be wondered at.– In such a position would your mind be perturbed or not?' Mencius replied, 'No. At forty, I attained to an unperturbed mind.'

2. Ch'âu said, 'Since it is so with you, my Master, you are far beyond Mang Pan.' 'The mere attainment,' said Mencius, 'is not difficult. The scholar Kâo had attained to an unperturbed mind at an earlier period of life than I did.'

3. Ch'âu asked, 'Is there any way to an unperturbed mind?' The answer was, 'Yes.

4. 'Pî-kung Yû had this way of nourishing his valour:– He did not flinch from any strokes at his body. He did not turn his eyes aside from any thrusts at them. He considered that the slightest push from any one was the same as if he were beaten before the crowds in the market-place, and that what he would not receive from a common man in his loose large garments of hair, neither should he receive from a prince of ten thousand chariots. He viewed stabbing a prince of ten thousand chariots just as stabbing a fellow dressed in cloth of hair. He feared not any of all the princes. A bad word addressed to him he always returned.

5. 'Mang Shih-shê had this way of nourishing his valour:– He said, "I look upon not conquering and conquering in the same way. To measure the enemy and then advance; to calculate the chances of victory and then engage:– this is to stand in awe of the opposing force. How can I make certain of conquering? I can only rise superior to all fear."

6. 'Mang Shih-shê resembled the philosopher Tsang. Pî-kung Yû resembled Tsze-hsiâ. I do not know to the valour of which of the two the superiority should be ascribed, but yet Mang Shih-shê attended to what was of the greater importance.

7. 'Formerly, the philosopher Tsang said to Tsze-hsiang, "Do you love valour? I heard an account of great valour from the Master. It speaks thus:– 'If, on self-examination, I find that I am not upright, shall I not be in fear even of a poor man in his loose garments of hair-cloth? If, on self-examination, I find that I am upright, I will go forward against thousands and tens of thousands.'"

8. Yet, what Mang Shih-shê maintained, being merely his physical energy, was after all inferior to what the philosopher Tsang maintained, which was indeed of the most importance.'

9. Kung-sun Ch'âu said, 'May I venture to ask an explanation from you, Master, of how you maintain an unperturbed mind, and how the philosopher Kâo does the same?' Mencius answered, 'Kâo says,– "What is not attained in words is not to be sought for in the mind; what produces dissatisfaction in the mind, is not to be helped by passion-effort." This last,– when there is unrest in the mind, not to seek for relief from passion-effort, may be conceded. But not to seek in the mind for what is not attained in words cannot be conceded. The will is the leader

of the passion-nature. The passion-nature pervades and animates the body. The will is first and chief, and the passion-nature is subordinate to it. Therefore I say,– Maintain firm the will, and do no violence to the passion-nature.'

10. Ch'âu observed, 'Since you say– "The will is chief, and the passion-nature is subordinate," how do you also say, "Maintain firm the will, and do no violence to the passion-nature?"' Mencius replied, 'When it is the will alone which is active, it moves the passion-nature. When it is the passion-nature alone which is active, it moves the will. For instance now, in the case of a man falling or running, that is from the passion-nature, and yet it moves the mind.'

11. 'I venture to ask,' said Ch'âu again, 'wherein you, Master, surpass Kâo.' Mencius told him, 'I understand words. I am skilful in nourishing my vast, flowing passion-nature.'

12. Ch'âu pursued, 'I venture to ask what you mean by your vast, flowing passion-nature!' The reply was, 'It is difficult to describe it.

13. 'This is the passion-nature:– It is exceedingly great, and exceedingly strong. Being nourished by rectitude, and sustaining no injury, it fills up all between heaven and earth.

14. 'This is the passion-nature:– It is the mate and assistant of righteousness and reason. Without it, man is in a state of starvation.

15. 'It is produced by the accumulation of righteous deeds; it is not to be obtained by incidental acts of righteousness. If the mind does not feel complacency in the conduct, the nature becomes starved. I therefore said, "Kâo has never understood righteousness, because he makes it something external."

16. 'There must be the constant practice of this righteousness, but without the object of thereby nourishing the passion-nature. Let not the mind forget its work, but let there be no assisting the growth of that nature. Let us not be like the man of Sung. There was a man of Sung, who was grieved that his growing corn was not longer, and so he pulled it up. Having done this, he returned home, looking very stupid, and said to his people, "I am tired to-day. I have been helping the corn to grow long." His son ran to look at it, and found the corn all withered. There are few in the world, who do not deal with their passion-nature, as if they were assisting the corn to grow long. Some indeed consider it of no benefit to them, and let it alone:– they do not weed their corn. They who assist it to grow long, pull out their corn. What they do is not only of no benefit to the nature, but it also injures it.'

17. Kung-sun Ch'âu further asked, 'What do you mean by saying that you understand whatever words you hear?' Mencius replied, 'When words are

one-sided, I know how the mind of the speaker is clouded over. When words are extravagant, I know how the mind is fallen and sunk. When words are all-depraved, I know how the mind has departed from principle. When words are evasive, I know how the mind is at its wit's end. These evils growing in the mind, do injury to government, and, displayed in the government, are hurtful to the conduct of affairs. When a Sage shall again arise, he will certainly follow my words.'

18. On this Ch'âu observed, 'Tsâi Wo and Tsze-kung were skilful in speaking. Zan Niû, the disciple Min, and Yen Yüan, while their words were good, were distinguished for their virtuous conduct. Confucius united the qualities of the disciples in himself, but still he said, "In the matter of speeches, I am not competent."– Then, Master, have you attained to be a Sage?'

19. Mencius said, 'Oh! what words are these? Formerly Tsze-kung asked Confucius, saying, "Master, are you a Sage?" Confucius answered him, "A Sage is what I cannot rise to. I learn without satiety, and teach without being tired." Tsze-kung said, "You learn without satiety:– that shows your wisdom. You teach without being tired:– that shows your benevolence. Benevolent and wise:– Master, you ARE a Sage." Now, since Confucius would not allow himself to be regarded as a Sage, what words were those?'

20. Ch'âu said, 'Formerly, I once heard this:– Tsze-hsiâ, Tsze-yû, and Tsze-chang had each one member of the Sage. Zan Niû, the disciple Min, and Yen Yüan had all the members, but in small proportions. I venture to ask,– With which of these are you pleased to rank yourself?'

21. Mencius replied, 'Let us drop speaking about these, if you please.'

22. Ch'âu then asked, 'What do you say of Po-î and Î Yin?' 'Their ways were different from mine,' said Mencius. 'Not to serve a prince whom he did not esteem, nor command a people whom he did not approve; in a time of good government to take office, and on the occurrence of confusion to retire:– this was the way of Po-î. To say– "Whom may I not serve? My serving him makes him my ruler. What people may I not command? My commanding them makes them my people." In a time of good government to take office, and when disorder prevailed, also to take office:– that was the way of Î Yin. When it was proper to go into office, then to go into it; when it was proper to keep retired from office, then to keep retired from it; when it was proper to continue in it long, then to continue in it long - when it was proper to withdraw from it quickly, then to withdraw quickly:– that was the way of Confucius. These were all sages of antiquity, and I have not attained to do what they did. But what I wish to do is to learn to be like Confucius.'

23. Ch'âu said, 'Comparing Po-î and Î Yin with Confucius, are they to be placed in the same rank?' Mencius replied, 'No. Since there were living men until now, there never was another Confucius.'

24. Ch'âu said, 'Then, did they have any points of agreement with him?' The reply was,– 'Yes. If they had been sovereigns over a hundred lî of territory, they would, all of them, have brought all the princes to attend in their court, and have obtained the throne. And none of them, in order to obtain the throne, would have committed one act of unrighteousness, or put to death one innocent person. In those things they agreed with him.'

25. Ch'âu said, 'I venture to ask wherein he differed from them.' Mencius replied, 'Tsâi Wo, Tsze-kung, and Yû Zo had wisdom sufficient to know the sage. Even had they been ranking themselves low, they would not have demeaned themselves to flatter their favourite.

26. 'Now, Tsâi Wo said, "According to my view of our Master, he was far superior to Yâo and Shun."

27. 'Tsze-kung said, "By viewing the ceremonial ordinances of a prince, we know the character of his government. By hearing his music, we know the character of his virtue. After the lapse of a hundred ages I can arrange, according to their merits, the kings of a hundred ages;– not one of them can escape me. From the birth of mankind till now, there has never been another like our Master."

28. 'Yû Zo said, "Is it only among men that it is so? There is the Ch'î-lin among quadrupeds, the Fang-hwang among birds, the T'âi mountain among mounds and ant-hills, and rivers and seas among rain-pools. Though different in degree, they are the same in kind. So the sages among mankind are also the same in kind. But they stand out from their fellows, and rise above the level, and from the birth of mankind till now, there never has been one so complete as Confucius."'

CHAPTER 6

1. Mencius said, 'He who, using force, makes a pretence to benevolence is the leader of the princes. A leader of the princes requires a large kingdom. He who, using virtue, practises benevolence is the sovereign of the kingdom. To become the sovereign of the kingdom, a prince need not wait for a large kingdom. T'ang did it with only seventy lî, and king Wan with only a hundred.

2. 'When one by force subdues men, they do not submit to him in heart. They submit, because their strength is not adequate to resist. When one subdues men by virtue, in their hearts' core they are pleased, and sincerely submit, as was the case with the seventy disciples in their submission to Confucius. What is said in the Book of Poetry:

> *From the west, from the east,*
> *From the south, from the north,*
> *There was not one who thought of refusing submission,*

is an illustration of this.'

•

1. Mencius said, 'Benevolence brings glory to a prince, and the opposite of it brings disgrace. For the princes of the present day to hate disgrace and yet to live complacently doing what is not benevolent, is like hating moisture and yet living in a low situation.

2. 'If a prince hates disgrace, the best course for him to pursue, is to esteem virtue and honour virtuous scholars, giving the worthiest among them places of dignity, and the able offices of trust. When throughout his kingdom there is leisure and rest from external troubles, let him, taking advantage of such a season, clearly digest the principles of his government with its legal sanctions, and then even great kingdoms will be constrained to stand in awe of him.

3. 'It is said in the Book of Poetry,

> *Before the heavens were dark with rain,*
> *I gathered the bark from the roots of the mulberry trees,*
> *And wove it closely to form the window and door of my nest;*
> *Now, I thought, ye people below,*
> *Perhaps ye will not dare to insult me.*

Confucius said, "Did not he who made this ode understand the way of governing?" If a prince is able rightly to govern his kingdom, who will dare to insult him?

4. 'But now the princes take advantage of the time when throughout their kingdoms there is leisure and rest from external troubles, to abandon themselves to pleasure and indolent indifference; they in fact seek for calamities for themselves.

5. 'Calamity and happiness in all cases are men's own seeking.

6. 'This is illustrated by what is said in the Book of Poetry:

Be always studious to be in harmony with the ordinances of God,
So you will certainly get for yourself much happiness;

and by the passage of the Tâi Chiah:

"*When Heaven sends down calamities, it is still possible to escape from them; when we occasion the calamities ourselves, it is not possible any longer to live.*"

•

1. Mencius said, 'If a ruler give honour to men of talents and virtue and employ the able, so that offices shall all be filled by individuals of distinction and mark;– then all the scholars of the kingdom will be pleased, and wish to stand in his court.

2. 'If, in the market-place of his capital, he levy a ground-rent on the shops but does not tax the goods, or enforce the proper regulations without levying a ground-rent;– then all the traders of the kingdom will be pleased, and wish to store their goods in his market-place.

3. 'If, at his frontier-passes, there be an inspection of persons, but no taxes charged on goods or other articles, then all the travellers of the kingdom will be pleased, and wish to make their tours on his roads.

4. 'If he require that the husbandmen give their mutual aid to cultivate the public feld, and exact no other taxes from them;– then all the husbandmen of the kingdom will be pleased, and wish to plough in his fields.

5. 'If from the occupiers of the shops in his market-place he do not exact the fine of the individual idler, or of the hamlet's quota of cloth, then all the people of the kingdom will be pleased, and wish to come and be his people.

6. 'If a ruler can truly practise these five things, then the people in the neighbouring kingdoms will look up to him as a parent. From the first birth of mankind till now, never has any one led children to attack their parent, and succeeded in his design. Thus, such a ruler will not have an enemy in all the kingdom, and he who has no enemy in the kingdom is the minister of Heaven. Never has there been a ruler in such a case who did not attain to the royal dignity.'

•

1. Mencius said, 'All men have a mind which cannot bear to see the sufferings of others.

2. 'The ancient kings had this commiserating mind, and they, as a matter of course, had likewise a commiserating government. When with a commiserating mind was practised a commiserating government, to rule the kingdom was as easy a matter as to make anything go round in the palm.

3. 'When I say that all men have a mind which cannot bear to see the sufferings of others, my meaning may be illustrated thus:– even now-a-days, if men suddenly see a child about to fall into a well, they will without exception experience a feeling of alarm and distress. They will feel so, not as a ground on which they may gain the favour of the child's parents, nor as a ground on which they may seek the praise of their neighbours and friends, nor from a dislike to the reputation of having been unmoved by such a thing.

4. 'From this case we may perceive that the feeling of commiseration is essential to man, that the feeling of shame and dislike is essential to man, that the feeling of modesty and complaisance is essential to man, and that the feeling of approving and disapproving is essential to man.

5. 'The feeling of commiseration is the principle of benevolence. The feeling of shame and dislike is the principle of righteousness. The feeling of modesty and complaisance is the principle of propriety. The feeling of approving and disapproving is the principle of knowledge.

6. 'Men have these four principles just as they have their four limbs. When men, having these four principles, yet say of themselves that they cannot develop them, they play the thief with themselves, and he who says of his prince that he cannot develop them plays the thief with his prince.

7. 'Since all men have these four principles in themselves, let them know to give them all their development and completion, and the issue will be like that of fire which has begun to burn, or that of a spring which has begun to find vent. Let them have their complete development, and they will suffice to love and protect all within the four seas. Let them be denied that development, and they will not suffice for a man to serve his parents with.'

•

1. Mencius said, 'Is the arrow-maker less benevolent than the maker of armour of defence? And yet, the arrow-maker's only fear is lest men should not be hurt, and the armour-maker's only fear is lest men should be hurt. So it is with the priest and the coffin-maker. The choice of a profession, therefore, is a thing in which great caution is required.

2. 'Confucius said, "It is virtuous manners which constitute the excellence of a neighbourhood. If a man, in selecting a residence, do not fix on one where such prevail, how can he be wise?" Now, benevolence is the most honourable

dignity conferred by Heaven, and the quiet home in which man should dwell. Since no one can hinder us from being so, if yet we are not benevolent;– this is being not wise.

3. 'From the want of benevolence and the want of wisdom will ensue the entire absence of propriety and righteousness;– he who is in such a case must be the servant of other men. To be the servant of men and yet ashamed of such servitude, is like a bowmaker's being ashamed to make bows, or an arrow-maker's being ashamed to make arrows.

4. 'If he be ashamed of his case, his best course is to practise benevolence.

5. 'The man who would be benevolent is like the archer. The archer adjusts himself and then shoots. If he misses, he does not murmur against those who surpass himself. He simply turns round and seeks the cause of his failure in himself.'

●

1. Mencius said, 'When any one told Tsze-lû that he had a fault, he rejoiced.

2. 'When Yü heard good words, he bowed to the speaker.

3. 'The great Shun had a still greater delight in what was good. He regarded virtue as the common property of himself and others, giving up his own way to follow that of others, and delighting to learn from others to practise what was good.

4. 'From the time when he ploughed and sowed, exercised the potter's art, and was a fisherman, to the time when he became emperor, he was continually learning from others.

5. 'To take example from others to practise virtue, is to help them in the same practice. Therefore, there is no attribute of the superior man greater than his helping men to practise virtue.'

●

1. Mencius said, 'Po-î would not serve a prince whom he did not approve, nor associate with a friend whom he did not esteem. He would not stand in a bad prince's court, nor speak with a bad man. To stand in a bad prince's court, or to speak with a bad man, would have been to him the same as to sit with his court robes and court cap amid mire and ashes. Pursuing the examination of his dislike to what was evil, we find that he thought it necessary, if he happened to be standing with a villager whose cap was not rightly adjusted, to leave him with a high air, as if he were going to be defiled. Therefore, although some of the princes made application to him with very proper messages, he would not receive their gifts.– He would not receive their gifts, counting it inconsistent with his purity to go to them.

2. 'Hûi of Liû-hsiâ was not ashamed to serve an impure prince, nor did he think it low to be an inferior officer. When advanced to employment, he did not conceal his virtue, but made it a point to carry out his principles. When neglected and left without office, he did not murmur. When straitened by poverty, he did not grieve. Accordingly, he had a saying,"You are you, and I am I. Although you stand by my side with breast and aims bare, or with your body naked, how can you defile me?" Therefore, self-possessed, he companied with men indifferently, at the same time not losing himself. When he wished to leave, if pressed to remain in office, he would remain.– He would remain in office, when pressed to do so, not counting it required by his purity to go away.'

3. Mencius said, 'Po-î was narrow-minded, and Hûi of Liû-hsiâ was wanting in self-respect. The superior man will not manifest either narrow-mindedness, or the want of self-respect.'

CHAPTER 7

1. Mencius said, 'Opportunities of time vouchsafed by Heaven are not equal to advantages of situation afforded by the Earth, and advantages of situation afforded by the Earth are not equal to the union arising from the accord of Men.

2. 'There is a city, with an inner wall of three lî in circumference, and an outer wall of seven.– The enemy surround and attack it, but they are not able to take it. Now, to surround and attack it, there must have been vouchsafed to them by Heaven the opportunity of time, and in such case their not taking it is because opportunities of time vouchsafed by Heaven are not equal to advantages of situation afforded by the Earth.

3. 'There is a city, whose walls are distinguished for their height, and whose moats are distinguished for their depth, where the arms of its defenders, offensive and defensive, are distinguished for their strength and sharpness, and the stores of rice and other grain are very large. Yet it is obliged to be given up and abandoned. This is because advantages of situation afforded by the Earth are not equal to the union arising from the accord of Men.

4. 'In accordance with these principles it is said, "A people is bounded in, not by the limits of dykes and borders; a State is secured, not by the strengths of mountains and rivers; the kingdom is overawed, not by the sharpness and strength of arms." He who finds the proper course has many to assist him. He who loses the proper course has few to assist him. When this,– the being assisted by few,– reaches its extreme point, his own relations revolt from the prince. When the being assisted by many reaches its highest point, the whole kingdom becomes obedient to the prince.

5. 'When one to whom the whole kingdom is prepared to be obedient, attacks those from whom their own relations revolt, what must be the result? Therefore, the true ruler will prefer not to fight; but if he does fight, he must overcome.'

•

1. As Mencius was about to go to court to see the king, the king sent a person to him with this message,– 'I was wishing to come and see you. But I have got a cold, and may not expose myself to the wind. In the morning I will hold my court. I do not know whether you will give me the opportunity of seeing you then.' Mencius replied, 'Unfortunately, I am unwell, and not able to go to the court.'

2. Next day, he went out to pay a visit of condolence to some one of the Tung-kwoh family, when Kung-sun Ch'âu said to him, 'Yesterday, you declined

going to the court on the ground of being unwell, and to-day you are going to pay a visit of condolence. May this not be regarded as improper?' 'Yesterday,' said Mencius, 'I was unwell; to-day, I am better:– why should I not pay this visit?'

3. In the mean time, the king sent a messenger to inquire about his sickness, and also a physician. Mang Chung replied to them, 'Yesterday, when the king's order came, he was feeling a little unwell, and could not go to the court. To-day he was a little better, and hastened to go to court. I do not know whether he can have reached it by this time or not.' Having said this, he sent several men to look for Mencius on the way, and say to him, 'I beg that, before you return home, you will go to the court.'

4. On this, Mencius felt himself compelled to go to Ching Ch'âu's, and there stop the night. Mr. Ching said to him, 'In the family, there is the relation of father and son; abroad, there is the relation of prince and minister. These are the two great relations among men. Between father and son the ruling principle is kindness. Between prince and minister the ruling principle is respect. I have seen the respect of the king to you, Sir, but I have not seen in what way you show respect to him.' Mencius replied, 'Oh! what words are these? Among the people of Ch'î there is no one who speaks to the king about benevolence and righteousness. Are they thus silent because they do not think that benevolence and righteousness are admirable? No, but in their hearts they say, "This man is not fit to be spoken with about benevolence and righteousness." Thus they manifest a disrespect than which there can be none greater. I do not dare to set forth before the king any but the ways of Yâo and Shun. There is therefore no man of Ch'î who respects the king so much as I do.'

5. Mr. Ching said, 'Not so. That was not what I meant. In the Book of Rites it is said, "When a father calls, the answer must be without a moment's hesitation. When the prince's order calls, the carriage must not be waited for." You were certainly going to the court, but when you heard the king's order, then you did not carry your purpose out. This does seem as if it were not in accordance with that rule of propriety.'

6. Mencius answered him, 'How can you give that meaning to my conduct? The philosopher Tsang said, "The wealth of Tsin and Ch'û cannot be equalled. Let their rulers have their wealth:– I have my benevolence. Let them have their nobility:– I have my righteousness. Wherein should I be dissatisfied as inferior to them?" Now shall we say that these sentiments are not right? Seeing that the philosopher Tsang spoke them, there is in them, I apprehend, a real principle.– In the kingdom there are three things universally acknowledged to be honourable. Nobility is one of them; age is one of them; virtue is one of them. In courts, nobility holds the first place of the three; in villages, age holds the first place; and

for helping one's generation and presiding over the people, the other two are not equal to virtue. How can the possession of only one of these be presumed on to despise one who possesses the other two?

7. 'Therefore a prince who is to accomplish great deeds will certainly have ministers whom he does not call to go to him. When he wishes to consult with them, he goes to them. The prince who does not honour the virtuous, and delight in their ways of doing, to this extent, is not worth having to do with.

8. 'Accordingly, there was the behaviour of T'ang to Î Yin:– he first learned of him, and then employed him as his minister; and so without difficulty he became sovereign. There was the behaviour of the duke Hwan to Kwan Chung:– he first learned of him, and then employed him as his minister; and so without difficulty he became chief of all the princes.

9. 'Now throughout the kingdom, the territories of the princes are of equal extent, and in their achievements they are on a level. Not one of them is able to exceed the others. This is from no other reason, but that they love to make ministers of those whom they teach, and do not love to make ministers of those by whom they might be taught.

10. 'So did T'ang behave to Î Yin, and the duke Hwan to Kwan Chung, that they would not venture to call them to go to them. If Kwan Chung might not be called to him by his prince, how much less may he be called, who would not play the part of Kwan Chung!'

•

1. Ch'an Tsin asked Mencius, saying, 'Formerly, when you were in Ch'î, the king sent you a present of 2,400 taels of fine silver, and you refused to accept it. When you were in Sung, 1,680 taels were sent to you, which you accepted; and when you were in Hsieh, 1,200 taels were sent, which you likewise accepted. If your declining to accept the gift in the first case was right, your accepting it in the latter cases was wrong. If your accepting it in the latter cases was right, your declining to do so in the first case was wrong. You must accept, Master, one of these alternatives.'

2. Mencius said, 'I did right in all the cases.

3. 'When I was in Sung, I was about to take a long journey. Travellers must be provided with what is necessary for their expenses. The prince's message was, 'A present against travelling-expenses." Why should I have declined the gift?

4. 'When I was in Hsieh, I was apprehensive for my safety, and taking measures for my protection. The message was, "I have heard that you are taking measures to protect yourself, and send this to help you in procuring arms." Why should I have declined the gift?

5. 'But when I was in Ch'i, I had no occasion for money. To send a man a gift when he has no occasion for it, is to bribe him. How is it possible that a superior man should be taken with a bribe?'

•

1. Mencius having gone to P'ing-lû, addressed the governor of it, saying, 'If one of your spearmen should lose his place in the ranks three times in one day, would you, Sir, put him to death or not?' 'I would not wait for three times to do so,' was the reply.

2. Mencius said, 'Well then, you, Sir, have likewise lost your place in the ranks many times. In bad calamitous years, and years of famine, the old and feeble of your people, who have been found lying in the ditches and water-channels, and the able-bodied, who have been scattered about to the four quarters, have amounted to several thousand.' The governor replied, 'That is a state of things in which it does not belong to me Chü-hsin to act.'

3. 'Here,' said Mencius, 'is a man who receives charge of the cattle and sheep of another, and undertakes to feed them for him;– of course he must search for pasture-ground and grass for them. If, after searching for those, he cannot find them, will he return his charge to the owner? or will he stand by and see them die?' 'Herein,' said the officer, 'I am guilty.'

4. Another day, Mencius had an audience of the king, and said to him, 'Of the governors of your Majesty's cities I am acquainted with five, but the only one of them who knows his faults is K'ung Chü-hsin.' He then repeated the conversation to the king, who said, 'In this matter, I am the guilty one.'

•

1. Mencius said to Ch'î Wâ, 'There seemed to be reason in your declining the governorship of Ling-ch'iû, and requesting to be appointed chief criminal judge, because the latter office would afford you the opportunity of speaking your views. Now several months have elapsed, and have you yet found nothing of which you might speak?'

2. On this, Ch'î Wâ remonstrated on some matter with the king, and, his counsel not being taken, resigned his office and went away.

3. The people of Ch'î said, 'In the course which he marked out for Ch'î Wâ he did well, but we do not know as to the course which he pursues for himself.'

4. His disciple Kung-tû told him these remarks.

5. Mencius said, 'I have heard that he who is in charge of an office, when he is prevented from fulfilling its duties, ought to take his departure, and that he on whom is the responsibility of giving his opinion, when he finds his words

unattended to, ought to do the same. But I am in charge of no office; on me devolves no duty of speaking out my opinion:– may not I therefore act freely and without any constraint, either in going forward or in retiring?'

•

1. Mencius, occupying the position of a high dignitary of T'se, went on a mission of condolence to T'ang. The King also sent Wang Hwan, the governor of Ka, as assistant commissioner. Wang Hwan, morning and evening, waited upon Mencius, who during all the way to T'ang and back, never spoke to him about the business of their mission.

2. Kung-sun Ch'âu. said to Mencius, 'The position of a high dignitary of Ch'î is not a small one; the road from Ch'î to T'ang is not short. How was it that during all the way there and back you never spoke to Hwan about the matters of your mission?'

Mencius replied, 'There were the proper officers who attended to them. What occasion had I to speak to him about them?'

CHAPTER 8

1. Mencius went from Ch'î to Lû to bury his mother. On his return to Ch'î, he stopped at Ying, where Ch'ung Yü begged to put a question to him, and said, 'Formerly, in ignorance of my incompetency, you employed me to superintend the making of the coffin. As you were then pressed by the urgency of the business, I did not venture to put any question to you. Now, however, I wish to take the liberty to submit the matter. The wood of the coffin, it appeared to me, was too good.'

2. Mencius replied, 'Anciently, there was no rule for the size of either the inner or the outer coffin. In middle antiquity, the inner coffin was made seven inches thick, and the outer one the same. This was done by all, from the sovereign to the common people, and not simply for the beauty of the appearance, but because they thus satisfied the natural feelings of their hearts.

3. 'If prevented by statutory regulations from making their coffins in this way, men cannot have the feeling of pleasure. If they have not the money to make them in this way, they cannot have the feeling of pleasure. When they were not prevented, and had the money, the ancients all used this style. Why should I alone not do so?

4. 'And moreover, is there no satisfaction to the natural feelings of a man, in preventing the earth from getting near to the bodies of his dead?

5. 'I have heard that the superior man will not for all the world be niggardly to his parents.'

•

1. Shan T'ung, on his own impulse, asked Mencius, saying, 'May Yen be smitten?' Mencius replied, 'It may. Tsze-k'wâi had no right to give Yen to another man, and Tsze-chih had no right to receive Yen from Tsze-k'wâi. Suppose there were an officer here, with whom you, Sir, were pleased, and that, without informing the king, you were privately to give to him your salary and rank; and suppose that this officer, also without the king's orders, were privately to receive them from you– would such a transaction be allowable? And where is the difference between the case of Yen and this?'

2. The people of Ch'î smote Yen. Some one asked Mencius, saying, 'Is it really the case that you advised Ch'î to smite Yen?' He replied, 'No. Shan T'ung asked me whether Yen might be smitten, and I answered him, "It may." They accordingly went and smote it. If he had asked me– "Who may smite it?" I would have answered him, "He who is the minister of Heaven may smite it." Suppose the case of a murderer, and that one asks me– "May this man be put

to death?" I will answer him– "He may." If he ask me– "Who may put him to death?" I will answer him, "The chief criminal judge may put him to death." But now with one Yen to smite another Yen:– how should I have advised this?'

•

1. The people of Yen having rebelled, the king of Ch'î said, 'I feel very much ashamed when I think of Mencius.'

2. Ch'an Chiâ said to him, 'Let not your Majesty be grieved. Whether does your Majesty consider yourself or Châu-kung the more benevolent and wise?' The king replied, 'Oh! what words are those?' 'The duke of Châu,' said Chiâ, 'appointed Kwan-shû to oversee the heir of Yin, but Kwan-shû with the power of the Yin State rebelled. If knowing that this would happen he appointed Kwan-shû, he was deficient in benevolence. If he appointed him, not knowing that it would happen, he was deficient in knowledge. If the duke of Châu was not completely benevolent and wise, how much less can your Majesty be expected to be so! I beg to go and see Mencius, and relieve your Majesty from that feeling.'

3. Ch'an Chiâ accordingly saw Mencius, and asked him, saying, 'What kind of man was the duke of Châu?' 'An ancient sage,' was the reply. 'Is it the fact, that he appointed Kwan-shû to oversee the heir of Yin, and that Kwan-shû with the State of Yin rebelled?' 'It is.' 'Did the duke of Châu know that he would rebel, and purposely appoint him to that office?' Mencius said, 'He did not know.' 'Then, though a sage, he still fell into error?' 'The duke of Châu,' answered Mencius, 'was the younger brother. Kwan-shû was his elder brother. Was not the error of Châu-kung in accordance with what is right?

4. 'Moreover, when the superior men of old had errors, they reformed them. The superior men of the present time, when they have errors, persist in them. The errors of the superior men of old were like eclipses of the sun and moon. All the people witnessed them, and when they had reformed them, all the people looked up to them with their former admiration. But do the superior men of the present day only persist in their errors? They go on to apologize for them likewise.'

•

1. Mencius gave up his office, and made arrangements for returning to his native State.

2. The king came to visit him, and said, 'Formerly, I wished to see you, but in vain. Then, I got the opportunity of being by your side, and all my court joyed exceedingly along with me. Now again you abandon me, and are returning home. I do not know if hereafter I may expect to have another opportunity of seeing you.' Mencius replied, 'I dare not request permission to visit you at any particular time, but, indeed, it is what I desire.'

3. Another day, the king said to the officer Shih, 'I wish to give Mencius a

house, somewhere in the middle of the kingdom, and to support his disciples with an allowance of 10,000 chung, that all the officers and the people may have such an example to reverence and imitate. Had you not better tell him this for me?'

4. Shih took advantage to convey this message by means of the disciple Ch'an, who reported his words to Mencius.

5. Mencius said, 'Yes; but how should the officer Shih know that the thing could not be? Suppose that I wanted to be rich, having formerly declined 100,000 chung, would my now accepting 10,000 be the conduct of one desiring riches?

6. 'Chî-sun said, "A strange man was Tsze-shû Î. He pushed himself into the service of government. His prince declining to employ him, he had to retire indeed, but he again schemed that his son or younger brother should be made a high officer. Who indeed is there of men but wishes for riches and honour? But he only, among the seekers of these, tried to monopolize the conspicuous mound.

7. 'Of old time, the market-dealers exchanged the articles which they had for others which they had not, and simply had certain officers to keep order among them. It happened that there was a mean fellow, who made it a point to look out for a conspicuous mound, and get up upon it. Thence he looked right and left, to catch in his net the whole gain of the market. The people all thought his conduct mean, and therefore they proceeded to lay a tax upon his wares. The taxing of traders took its rise from this mean fellow."'

•

1. Mencius, having taken his leave of Ch'î, was passing the night in Châu.

2. A person who wished to detain him on behalf of the king, came and sat down, and began to speak to him. Mencius gave him no answer, but leant upon his stool and slept.

3. The visitor was displeased, and said, 'I passed the night in careful vigil, before I would venture to speak to you, and you, Master, sleep and do not listen to me. Allow me to request that I may not again presume to see you.' Mencius replied, 'Sit down, and I will explain the case clearly to you. Formerly, if the duke Mû had not kept a person by the side of Tsze-sze, he could not have induced Tsze-sze to remain with him. If Hsieh Liû and Shan Hsiang had not had a remembrancer by the side of the duke Mû, he would not have been able to make them feel at home and remain with him.

4. 'You anxiously form plans with reference to me, but you do not treat me as Tsze-sze was treated. Is it you, Sir, who cut me? Or is it I who cut you?

•

1. When Mencius had left Ch'î, Yin Shih spoke about him to others, saying, 'If he did not know that the king could not be made a T'ang or a Wû, that showed

his want of intelligence. If he knew that he could not be made such, and came notwithstanding, that shows he was seeking his own benefit. He came a thousand lî to wait on the king; because he did not find in him a ruler to suit him, he took his leave, but how dilatory and lingering was his departure, stopping three nights before he quitted Châu! I am dissatisfied on account of this.'

2. The disciple Kâo informed Mencius of these remarks.

3. Mencius said, 'How should Yin Shih know me! When I came a thousand lî to wait on the king, it was what I desired to do. When I went away because I did not find in him a ruler to suit me, was that what I desired to do? I felt myself constrained to do it.

4. 'When I stopped three nights before I quitted Châu, in my own mind I still considered my departure speedy. I was hoping that the king might change. If the king had changed, he would certainly have recalled me.

5. 'When I quitted Châu, and the king had not sent after me, then, and not till then, was my mind resolutely bent on returning to Tsâu. But, notwithstanding that, how can it be said that I give up the king? The king, after all, is one who may be made to do what is good If he were to use me, would it be for the happiness of the people of Ch'î only? It would be for the happiness of the people of the whole kingdom. I am hoping that the king will change. I am daily hoping for this.

6. 'Am I like one of your little-minded people? They will remonstrate with their prince, and on their remonstrance not being accepted, they get angry; and, with their passion displayed in their countenance, they take their leave, and travel with all their strength for a whole day, before they will stop for the night.'

7. When Yin Shih heard this explanation, he said, 'I am indeed a small man.'

•

1. When Mencius left Ch'î, Ch'ung Yü questioned him upon the way, saying, 'Master, you look like one who carries an air of dissatisfaction in his countenance. But formerly I heard you say– "The superior man does not murmur against Heaven, nor grudge against men."'

2. Mencius said, 'That was one time, and this is another.

3. 'It is a rule that a true royal sovereign should arise in the course of five hundred years, and that during that time there should be men illustrious in their generation.

4. 'From the commencement of the Châu dynasty till now, more than seven hundred years have elapsed. Judging numerically, the date is past. Examining the character of the present time, we might expect the rise of such individuals in it.

5. 'But Heaven does not yet wish that the kingdom should enjoy tranquillity and good order. If it wished this, who is there besides me to bring it about? How should I be otherwise than dissatisfied?'

1. When Mencius left Ch'î, he dwelt in Hsiû. There Kung-sun Ch'âu asked him, saying, 'Was it the way of the ancients to hold office without receiving salary?'

2. Mencius replied, 'No; when I first saw the king in Ch'ung, it was my intention, on retiring from the interview, to go away. Because I did not wish to change this intention, I declined to receive any salary.

3. 'Immediately after, there came orders for the collection of troops, when it would have been improper for me to beg permission to leave. But to remain so long in Ch'î was not my purpose.'

CHAPTER 9

1. When the prince, afterwards duke Wan of T'ang, had to go to Ch'û, he went by way of Sung, and visited Mencius.

2. Mencius discoursed to him how the nature of man is good, and when speaking, always made laudatory reference to Yâo and Shun.

3. When the prince was returning from Ch'û, he again visited Mencius. Mencius said to him, 'Prince, do you doubt my words? The path is one, and only one.

4. 'Ch'ang Chi'en said to duke King of Ch'î, "They were men. I am a man. Why should I stand in awe of them?" Yen Yüan said, "What kind of man was Shun? What kind of man am I? He who exerts himself will also become such as he was." Kung-Ming Î said, "King Wan is my teacher. How should the duke of Châu deceive me by those words?"

5. 'Now, T'ang, taking its length with its breadth, will amount, I suppose, to fifty lî. It is small, but still sufficient to make a good State. It is said in the Book of History, "If medicine do not raise a commotion in the patient, his disease will not be cured by it."'

●

1. When the duke Ting of T'ang died, the prince said to Yen Yû, 'Formerly, Mencius spoke with me in Sung, and in my mind I have never forgotten his words. Now, alas! this great duty to my father devolves upon me; I wish to send you to ask the advice of Mencius, and then to proceed to its various services'

2. Zan Yû accordingly proceeded to Tsâu, and consulted Mencius. Mencius said, 'Is this not good? In discharging the funeral duties to parents, men indeed feel constrained to do their utmost. The philosopher Tsang said, "When parents are alive, they should be served according to propriety; when they are dead, they should be buried according to propriety; and they should be sacrificed to according to propriety:– this may be called filial piety." The ceremonies to be observed by the princes I have not learned, but I have heard these points:– that the three years' mourning, the garment of coarse cloth with its lower edge even, and the eating of congee, were equally prescribed by the three dynasties, and binding on all, from the sovereign to the mass of the people.'

3. Zan Yû reported the execution of his commission, and the prince determined that the three years' mourning should be observed. His aged relatives, and the body of the officers, did not wish that it should be so, and said, 'The former princes of Lû, that kingdom which we honour, have, none of them, observed this practice, neither have any of our own former princes observed it. For you to act contrary to their example is not proper. Moreover, the History says,– "In the

observances of mourning and sacrifice, ancestors are to be followed," meaning that they received those things from a proper source to hand them down.'

4. The prince said again to Zan Yû, 'Hitherto, I have not given myself to the pursuit of learning, but have found my pleasure in horsemanship and sword-exercise, and now I don't come up to the wishes of my aged relatives and the officers. I am afraid I may not be able to discharge my duty in the great business that I have entered on; do you again consult Mencius for me.' On this, Zan Yû went again to Tsâu, and consulted Mencius. Mencius said, 'It is so, but he may not seek a remedy in others, but only in himself. Confucius said, "When a prince dies, his successor entrusts the administration to the prime minister. He sips the congee. His face is of a deep black. He approaches the place of mourning, and weeps. Of all the officers and inferior ministers there is not one who will presume not to join in the lamentation, he setting them this example. What the superior loves, his inferiors will be found to love exceedingly. The relation between superiors and inferiors is like that between the wind and grass. The grass must bend when the wind blows upon it." The business depends on the prince.'

5. Zan Yû returned with this answer to his commission, and the prince said, 'It is so. The matter does indeed depend on me.' So for five months he dwelt in the shed, without issuing an order or a caution. All the officers and his relatives said, 'He may be said to understand the ceremonies.' When the time of interment arrived, they came from all quarters of the State to witness it. Those who had come from other States to condole with him, were greatly pleased with the deep dejection of his countenance and the mournfulness of his wailing and weeping.

●

1. The duke Wan of T'ang asked Mencius about the proper way of governing a kingdom.

2. Mencius said, 'The business of the people may not be remissly attended to. It is said in the Book of Poetry,

> *In the day-light go and gather the grass,*
> *And at night twist your ropes;*
> *Then get up quickly on the roofs;–*
> *Soon must we begin sowing again the grain.*

3. 'The way of the people is this:– If they have a certain livelihood, they will have a fixed heart; if they have not a certain livelihood, they have not a fixed heart. If they have not a fixed heart, there is nothing which they will not do in the way of self-abandonment, of moral deflection, of depravity, and of wild license. When they have thus been involved in crime, to follow them up and punish them:– this is to entrap the people. How can such a thing as entrapping the people be done under the rule of a benevolent man?

4. 'Therefore, a ruler who is endowed with talents and virtue will be gravely complaisant and economical, showing a respectful politeness to his ministers, and taking from the people only in accordance with regulated limits.

5. 'Yang Hû said, "He who seeks to be rich will not be benevolent. He who wishes to be benevolent will not be rich."

6. 'The sovereign of the Hsiâ dynasty enacted the fifty mâu allotment, and the payment of a tax. The founder of the Yin enacted the seventy mâu allotment, and the system of mutual aid. The founder of the Châu enacted the hundred mâu allotment, and the share system. In reality, what was paid in all these was a tithe. The share system means mutual division. The aid system means mutual dependence.

7. 'Lung said, "For regulating the lands, there is no better system than that of mutual aid, and none which is not better than that of taxing. By the tax system, the regular amount was fixed by taking the average of several years. In good years, when the grain lies about in abundance, much might be taken without its being oppressive, and the actual exaction would be small. But in bad years, the produce being not sufficient to repay the manuring of the fields, this system still requires the taking of the full amount. When the parent of the people causes the people to wear looks of distress, and, after the whole year's toil, yet not to be able to nourish their parents, so that they proceed to borrowing to increase their means, till the old people and children are found lying in the ditches and water-channels:– where, in such a case, is his parental relation to the people?"

8. 'As to the system of hereditary salaries, that is already observed in T'ang.

9. 'It is said in the Book of Poetry,

> *May the rain come down on our public field,*
> *And then upon our private fields!*

It is only in the system of mutual aid that there is a public field, and from this passage we perceive that even in the Châu dynasty this system has been recognised.

10. 'Establish hsiang, hsü, hsio, and hsiâo,– all those educational institutions,– for the instruction of the people. The name hsiang indicates nourishing as its object; hsiâo, indicates teaching: and hsü indicates archery. By the Hsiâ dynasty the name hsiâo was used; by the Yin, that of hsü; and by the Châu, that of hsiang. As to the hsio, they belonged to the three dynasties, and by that name. The object of them all is to illustrate the human relations. When those are thus illustrated by superiors, kindly feeling will prevail among the inferior people below.

11. 'Should a real sovereign arise, he will certainly come and take an example from you; and thus you will be the teacher of the true sovereign.

12. 'It is said in the Book of Poetry,

Although Châu was an old country,
It received a new destiny.

That is said with reference to king Wan. Do you practise those things with vigour, and you also will by them make new your kingdom.'

13. The duke afterwards sent Pî Chan to consult Mencius about the nine-squares system of dividing the land. Mencius said to him, 'Since your prince, wishing to put in practice a benevolent government, has made choice of you and put you into this employment, you must exert yourself to the utmost. Now, the first thing towards a benevolent government must be to lay down the boundaries. If the boundaries be not defined correctly, the division of the land into squares will not be equal, and the produce available for salaries will not be evenly distributed. On this account, oppressive rulers and impure ministers are sure to neglect this defining of the boundaries. When the boundaries have been defined correctly, the division of the fields and the regulation of allowances may be determined by you, sitting at your ease.

14. 'Although the territory of T'ang is narrow and small, yet there must be in it men of a superior grade, and there must be in it country-men. If there were not men of a superior grade, there would be none to rule the country-men. If there were not country-men, there would be none to support the men of superior grade.

15. 'I would ask you, in the remoter districts, observing the nine-squares division, to reserve one division to be cultivated on the system of mutual aid, and in the more central parts of the kingdom, to make the people pay for themselves a tenth part of their produce.

16. 'From the highest officers down to the lowest, each one must have his holy field, consisting of fifty mâu.

17. 'Let the supernumerary males have their twenty-five mâu.

18. 'On occasions of death, or removal from one dwelling to another, there will be no quitting the district. In the fields of a district, those who belong to the same nine squares render all friendly offices to one another in their going out and coming in, aid one another in keeping watch and ward, and sustain one another in sickness. Thus the people are brought to live in affection and harmony.

19. 'A square lî covers nine squares of land, which nine squares contain nine hundred mâu. The central square is the public field, and eight families, each having its private hundred mâu, cultivate in common the public field. And not till the public work is finished, may they presume to attend to their private affairs. This is the way by which the country-men are distinguished from those of a superior grade.

20. 'Those are the great outlines of the system. Happily to modify and adapt it depends on the prince and you.'

CHAPTER 10

1. There came from Ch'û to T'ang one Hsü Hsing, who gave out that he acted according to the words of Shan-nang. Coming right to his gate, he addressed the duke Wan, saying, 'A man of a distant region, I have heard that you, Prince, are practising a benevolent government, and I wish to receive a site for a house, and to become one of your people.' The duke Wan gave him a dwelling-place. His disciples, amounting to several tens, all wore clothes of haircloth, and made sandals of hemp and wove mats for a living.

2. At the same time, Ch'an Hsiang, a disciple of Ch'an Liang, and his younger brother, Hsin, with their plough-handles and shares on their backs, came from Sung to T'ang, saying, 'We have heard that you, Prince, are putting into practice the government of the ancient sages, showing that you are likewise a sage. We wish to become the subjects of a sage.'

3. When Ch'an Hsiang saw Hsü Hsing, he was greatly pleased with him, and, abandoning entirely whatever he had learned, became his disciple. Having an interview with Mencius, he related to him with approbation the words of Hsü Hsing to the following effect:– 'The prince of T'ang is indeed a worthy prince. He has not yet heard, however, the real doctrines of antiquity. Now, wise and able princes should cultivate the ground equally and along with their people, and eat the fruit of their labour. They should prepare their own meals, morning and evening, while at the same time they carry on their government. But now, the prince of T'ang has his granaries, treasuries, and arsenals, which is an oppressing of the people to nourish himself. How can he be deemed a real worthy prince?'

4. Mencius said,'I suppose that Hsü Hsing sows grain and eats the produce. Is it not so?' 'It is so,' was the answer. 'I suppose also he weaves cloth, and wears his own manufacture. Is it not so?' 'No. Hsü wears clothes of haircloth.' 'Does he wear a cap?' 'He wears a cap.' 'What kind of cap?' 'A plain cap.' 'Is it woven by himself?' 'No. He gets it in exchange for grain.' 'Why does Hsü not weave it himself?' 'That would injure his husbandry.' 'Does Hsü cook his food in boilers and earthenware pans, and does he plough with an iron share?' 'Yes.' 'Does he make those articles himself?' 'No He gets them in exchange for grain.'

5. Mencius then said, 'The getting those various articles in exchange for grain, is not oppressive to the potter and the founder, and the potter and the founder in their turn, in exchanging their various articles for grain, are not oppressive to the husbandman. How should such a thing be supposed? And moreover, why does not Hsü act the potter and founder, supplying himself with the articles which he

uses solely from his own establishment? Why does he go confusedly dealing and exchanging with the handicraftsmen? Why does he not spare himself so much trouble?' Ch'an Hsiang replied, 'The business of the handicraftsman can by no means be carried on along with the business of husbandry.'

6. Mencius resumed, 'Then, is it the government of the kingdom which alone can be carried on along with the practice of husbandry? Great men have their proper business, and little men have their proper business. Moreover, in the case of any single individual, whatever articles he can require are ready to his hand, being produced by the various handicraftsmen:– if he must first make them for his own use, this way of doing would keep all the people running about upon the roads. Hence, there is the saying, "Some labour with their minds, and some labour with their strength. Those who labour with their minds govern others; those who labour with their strength are governed by others. Those who are governed by others support them; those who govern others are supported by them." This is a principle universally recognised.

7. 'In the time of Yâo, when the world had not yet been perfectly reduced to order, the vast waters, flowing out of their channels, made a universal inundation. Vegetation was luxuriant, and birds and beasts swarmed. The various kinds of grain could not be grown. The birds and beasts pressed upon men. The paths marked by the feet of beasts and prints of birds crossed one another throughout the Middle Kingdom. To Yâo alone this caused anxious sorrow. He raised Shun to office, and measures to regulate the disorder were set forth. Shun committed to Yî the direction of the fire to be employed, and Yî set fire to, and consumed, the forests and vegetation on the mountains and in the marshes, so that the birds and beasts fled away to hide themselves. Yü separated the nine streams, cleared the courses of the Tsî and T'â, and led them all to the sea. He opened a vent also for the Zû and Han, and regulated the course of the Hwâ'i and Sze, so that they all flowed into the Chiang. When this was done, it became possible for the people of the Middle Kingdom to cultivate the ground and get food for themselves. During that time, Yü was eight years away from his home, and though he thrice passed the door of it, he did not enter. Although he had wished to cultivate the ground, could he have done so?'

8. 'The Minister of Agriculture taught the people to sow and reap, cultivating the five kinds of grain. When the five kinds of grain were brought to maturity, the people all obtained a subsistence. But men possess a moral nature; and if they are well fed, warmly clad, and comfortably lodged, without being taught at the same time, they become almost like the beasts. This was a subject of anxious solicitude to the sage Shun, and he appointed Hsieh to be the Minister of Instruction, to teach the relations of humanity:– how, between father and

son, there should be affection; between sovereign and minister, righteousness; between husband and wife, attention to their separate functions; between old and young, a proper order; and between friends, fidelity. The high meritorious sovereign said to him, "Encourage them; lead them on; rectify them; straighten them; help them; give them wings:– thus causing them to become possessors of themselves. Then follow this up by stimulating them, and conferring benefits on them." When the sages were exercising their solicitude for the people in this way, had they leisure to cultivate the ground?

9. 'What Yâo felt giving him anxiety was the not getting Shun. What Shun felt giving him anxiety was the not getting Yü and Kâo Yâo. But he whose anxiety is about his hundred mâu not being properly cultivated, is a mere husbandman.

10. 'The imparting by a man to others of his wealth, is called "kindness." The teaching others what is good, is called "the exercise of fidelity." The finding a man who shall benefit the kingdom, is called "benevolence." Hence to give the throne to another man would be easy; to find a man who shall benefit the kingdom is difficult.

11. 'Confucius said, "Great indeed was Yâo as a sovereign. It is only Heaven that is great, and only Yâo corresponded to it. How vast was his virtue! The people could find no name for it. Princely indeed was Shun! How majestic was he, having possession of the kingdom, and yet seeming as if it were nothing to him!" In their governing the kingdom, were there no subjects on which Yâo and Shun employed their minds? There were subjects, only they did not employ their minds on the cultivation of the ground.

12. 'I have heard of men using the doctrines of our great land to change barbarians, but I have never yet heard of any being changed by barbarians. Ch'an Liang was a native of Ch'û. Pleased with the doctrines of Châu-kung and Chung-ne, he came northwards to the Middle Kingdom and studied them. Among the scholars of the northern regions, there was perhaps no one who excelled him. He was what you call a scholar of high and distinguished qualities. You and your brother followed him some tens of years, and when your master died, you forthwith turned away from him.

13. 'Formerly, when Confucius died, after three years had elapsed, his disciples collected their baggage, and prepared to return to their several homes. But on entering to take their leave of Tsze-kung, as they looked towards one another, they wailed, till they all lost their voices. After this they returned to their homes, but Tsze-kung went back, and built a house for himself on the altar-ground, where he lived alone other three years, before he returned home. On another occasion, Tsze-hsiâ, Tsze-chang, and Tsze-yû, thinking that Yû Zo

resembled the sage, wished to render to him the same observances which they had rendered to Confucius. They tried to force the disciple Tsang to join with them, but he said, "This may not be done. What has been washed in the waters of the Chiang and Han, and bleached in the autumn sun:– how glistening is it! Nothing can be added to it."

14. 'Now here is this shrike-tongued barbarian of the south, whose doctrines are not those of the ancient kings. You turn away from your master and become his disciple. Your conduct is different indeed from that of the philosopher Tsang.

15. 'I have heard of birds leaving dark valleys to remove to lofty trees, but I have not heard of their descending from lofty trees to enter into dark valleys.

16. 'In the Praise-songs of Lû it is said,

> He smote the barbarians of the west and the north,
> He punished Ching and Shû.

Thus Châu-kung would be sure to smite them, and you become their disciple again; it appears that your change is not good.'

17. Ch'an Hsiang said, 'If Hsü's doctrines were followed, then there would not be two prices in the market, nor any deceit in the kingdom. If a boy of five cubits were sent to the market, no one would impose on him; linen and silk of the same length would be of the same price. So it would be with bundles of hemp and silk, being of the same weight; with the different kinds of grain, being the same in quantity; and with shoes which were of the same size.'

18. Mencius replied, 'It is the nature of things to be of unequal quality. Some are twice, some five times, some ten times, some a hundred times, some a thousand times, some ten thousand times as valuable as others. If you reduce them all to the same standard, that must throw the kingdom into confusion. If large shoes and small shoes were of the same price, who would make them? For people to follow the doctrines of Hsü, would be for them to lead one another on to practise deceit. How can they avail for the government of a State?'

•

1. The Mohist, Î Chih, sought, through Hsü Pî, to see Mencius. Mencius said, 'I indeed wish to see him, but at present I am still unwell. When I am better, I will myself go and see him. He need not come here again.'

2. Next day, Î Chih again sought to see Mencius. Mencius said, 'To-day I am able to see him. But if I do not correct his errors, the true principles will not be fully evident. Let me first correct him. I have heard that this Î is a Mohist. Now Mo considers that in the regulation of funeral matters a spare simplicity should be the rule. Î thinks with Mo's doctrines to change the customs of the

kingdom;– how does he regard them as if they were wrong, and not honour them? Notwithstanding his views, Î buried his parents in a sumptuous manner, and so he served them in the way which his doctrines discountenance.'

3. The disciple Hsü informed Î of these remarks. Î said, 'Even according to the principles of the learned, we find that the ancients acted towards the people "as if they were watching over an infant." What does this expression mean? To me it sounds that we are to love all without difference of degree; but the manifestation of love must begin with our parents.' Hsü reported this reply to Mencius, who said, 'Now, does Î really think that a man's affection for the child of his brother is merely like his affection for the infant of a neighbour? What is to be approved in that expression is simply this:– that if an infant crawling about is likely to fall into a well, it is no crime in the infant. Moreover, Heaven gives birth to creatures in such a way that they have one root, and Î makes them to have two roots. This is the cause of his error.

4. 'And, in the most ancient times, there were some who did not inter their parents. When their parents died, they took them up and threw them into some water-channel. Afterwards, when passing by them, they saw foxes and wild-cats devouring them, and flies and gnats biting at them. The perspiration started out upon their foreheads, and they looked away, unable to bear the sight. It was not on account of other people that this perspiration flowed. The emotions of their hearts affected their faces and eyes, and instantly they went home, and came back with baskets and spades and covered the bodies. If the covering them thus was indeed right, you may see that the filial son and virtuous man, in interring in a handsome manner their parents, act according to a proper rule.'

5. The disciple Hsü informed Î of what Mencius had said. Î was thoughtful for a short time, and then said, 'He has instructed me.'

53

CHAPTER 11

1. Ch'an Tâi said to Mencius, 'In not going to wait upon any of the princes, you seem to me to be standing on a small point. If now you were once to wait upon them, the result might be so great that you would make one of them sovereign, or, if smaller, that you would make one of them chief of all the other princes. Moreover, the History says, "By bending only one cubit, you make eight cubits straight." It appears to me like a thing which might be done.'

2. Mencius said, 'Formerly, the duke Ching of Ch'î, once when he was hunting, called his forester to him by a flag. The forester would not come, and the duke was going to kill him. With reference to this incident, Confucius said, "The determined officer never forgets that his end may be in a ditch or a stream; the brave officer never forgets that he may lose his head." What was it in the forester that Confucius thus approved? He approved his not going to the duke, when summoned by the article which was not appropriate to him. If one go to see the princes without waiting to be invited, what can be thought of him?

3. 'Moreover, that sentence, "By bending only one cubit, you make eight cubits straight," is spoken with reference to the gain that may be got. If gain be the object, then, if it can be got by bending eight cubits to make one cubit straight, may we likewise do that?

4. 'Formerly, the officer Châo Chien made Wang Liang act as charioteer for his favourite Hsî, when, in the course of a whole day, they did not get a single bird. The favourite Hsî reported this result, saying, "He is the poorest charioteer in the world." Some one told this to Wang Liang, who said, "I beg leave to try again." By dint of pressing, this was accorded to him, when in one morning they got ten birds. The favourite, reporting this result, said, "He is the best charioteer in the world." Chien said, "I will make him always drive your chariot for you." When he told Wang Liang so, however, Liang refused, saying, "I drove for him, strictly observing the proper rules for driving, and in the whole day he did not get one bird. I drove for him so as deceitfully to intercept the birds, and in one morning he got ten. It is said in the Book of Poetry,

There is no failure in the management of their horses;
The arrows are discharged surely, like the blows of an axe.

I am not accustomed to drive for a mean man. I beg leave to decline the office."

5. 'Thus this charioteer even was ashamed to bend improperly to the will of such an archer. Though, by bending to it, they would have caught birds and animals

sufficient to form a hill, he would not do so. If I were to bend my principles and follow those princes, of what kind would my conduct be? And you are wrong. Never has a man who has bent himself been able to make others straight.'

●

1. King Ch'un said to Mencius "Are not Kung-sun Yen and Chang I really great men? Let them once be angry and all the princes are afraid. Let them live quietly, and the flames of trouble are extinguished throughout the empire".

2. Mencius said, 'How can such men be great men? Have you not read the Ritual Usages?– "At the capping of a young man, his father admonishes him. At the marrying away of a young woman, her mother admonishes her, accompanying her to the door on her leaving, and cautioning her with these words, 'You are going to your home. You must be respectful; you must be careful. Do not disobey your husband.'" Thus, to look upon compliance as their correct course is the rule for women.

3. 'To dwell in the wide house of the world, to stand in the correct seat of the world, and to walk in the great path of the world; when he obtains his desire for office, to practise his principles for the good of the people; and when that desire is disappointed, to practise them alone; to be above the power of riches and honours to make dissipated, of poverty and mean condition to make swerve from principle, and of power and force to make bend:– these characteristics constitute the great man.'

●

1. Châu Hsiâo asked Mencius, saying, 'Did superior men of old time take office?' Mencius replied, 'They did. The Record says, "If Confucius was three months without being employed by some ruler, he looked anxious and unhappy. When he passed from the boundary of a State, he was sure to carry with him his proper gift of introduction." Kung-ming Î said, "Among the ancients, if an officer was three months unemployed by a ruler, he was condoled with."'

2. Hsiâo said, 'Did not this condoling, on being three months unemployed by a ruler, show a too great urgency?'

3. Mencius answered, 'The loss of his place to an officer is like the loss of his State to a prince. It is said in the Book of Rites, "A prince ploughs himself, and is assisted by the people, to supply the millet for sacrifice. His wife keeps silkworms, and unwinds their cocoons, to make the garments for sacrifice." If the victims be not perfect, the millet not pure, and the dress not complete, he does not presume to sacrifice. "And the scholar who, out of office, has no holy field, in the same way, does not sacrifice. The victims for slaughter, the vessels, and the garments, not being all complete, he does not presume to sacrifice, and

then neither may he dare to feel happy." Is there not here sufficient ground also for condolence?'

4. Hsiâo again asked, 'What was the meaning of Confucius's always carrying his proper gift of introduction with him, when he passed over the boundaries of the State where he had been?'

5. 'An officer's being in office,' was the reply, 'is like the ploughing of a husbandman. Does a husbandman part with his plough, because he goes from one State to another?'

6. Hsiâo pursued, 'The kingdom of Tsin is one, as well as others, of official employments, but I have not heard of anyone being thus earnest about being in office. If there should be this urge why does a superior man make any difficulty about taking it?' Mencius answered, 'When a son is born, what is desired for him is that he may have a wife; when a daughter is born, what is desired for her is that she may have a husband. This feeling of the parents is possessed by all men. If the young people, without waiting for the orders of their parents, and the arrangements of the go-betweens, shall bore holes to steal a sight of each other, or get over the wall to be with each other, then their parents and all other people will despise them. The ancients did indeed always desire to be in office, but they also hated being so by any improper way. To seek office by an improper way is of a class with young people's boring holes.'

•

1. P'ang Kang asked Mencius, saying, 'Is it not an extravagant procedure to go from one prince to another and live upon them, followed by several tens of carriages, and attended by several hundred men?' Mencius replied, 'If there be not a proper ground for taking it, a single bamboo-cup of rice may not be received from a man. If there be such a proper ground, then Shun's receiving the kingdom from Yâo is not to be considered excessive. Do you think it was excessive?'

2. Kang said, 'No. But for a scholar performing no service to receive his support notwithstanding is improper.'

3. Mencius answered, 'If you do not have an intercommunication of the productions of labour, and an interchange of men's services, so that one from his overplus may supply the deficiency of another, then husbandmen will have a superfluity of grain, and women will have a superfluity of cloth. If you have such an interchange, carpenters and carriage-wrights may all get their food from you. Here now is a man, who, at home, is filial, and abroad, respectful to his elders; who watches over the principles of the ancient kings, awaiting the rise of future learners:– and yet you will refuse to support him. How is it that you give honour

to the carpenter and carriage-wright, and slight him who practises benevolence and righteousness?'

4. P'ang Kang said, 'The aim of the carpenter and carriagewright is by their trades to seek for a living. Is it also the aim of the superior man in his practice of principles thereby to seek for a living?' 'What have you to do,' returned Mencius, 'with his purpose? He is of service to you. He deserves to be supported, and should be supported. And let me ask,– Do you remunerate a man's intention, or do you remunerate his service.' To this Kang replied, 'I remunerate his intention.'

5. Mencius said, 'There is a man here, who breaks your tiles, and draws unsightly figures on your walls;– his purpose may be thereby to seek for his living, but will you indeed remunerate him?' 'No,' said Kang; and Mencius then concluded, 'That being the case, it is not the purpose which you remunerate, but the work done.'

•

1. Wan Chang asked Mencius, saying, 'Sung is a small State. Its ruler is now setting about to practise the true royal government, and Ch'î and Ch'û hate and attack him. What in this case is to be done?'

2. Mencius replied, 'When T'ang dwelt in Po, he adjoined to the State of Ko, the chief of which was living in a dissolute state and neglecting his proper sacrifices. T'ang sent messengers to inquire why he did not sacrifice. He replied, "I have no means of supplying the necessary victims." On this, T'ang caused oxen and sheep to be sent to him, but he ate them, and still continued not to sacrifice. T'ang again sent messengers to ask him the same question as before, when he replied, "I have no means of obtaining the necessary millet." On this, T'ang sent the mass of the people of Po to go and till the ground for him, while the old and feeble carried their food to them. The chief of Ko led his people to intercept those who were thus charged with wine, cooked rice, millet, and paddy, and took their stores from them, while they killed those who refused to give them up. There was a boy who had some millet and flesh for the labourers, who was thus slain and robbed. What is said in the Book of History, "The chief of Ko behaved as an enemy to the provision-carriers," has reference to this.

3. 'Because of his murder of this boy, T'ang proceeded to punish him. All within the four seas said, "It is not because he desires the riches of the kingdom, but to avenge a common man and woman."

4. 'When T'ang began his work of executing justice, he commenced with Ko, and though he made eleven punitive expeditions, he had not an enemy in the kingdom. When he pursued his work in the east, the rude tribes in the west murmured. So did those on the north, when he was engaged in the south. Their

cry was– "Why does he make us last." Thus, the people's longing for him was like their longing for rain in a time of great drought. The frequenters of the markets stopped not. Those engaged in weeding in the fields made no change in their operations. While he punished their rulers, he consoled the people. His progress was like the falling of opportune rain, and the people were delighted. It is said in the Book of History, "We have waited for our prince. When our prince comes, we may escape from the punishments under which we suffer."

5. 'There being some who would not become the subjects of Châu, king Wû proceeded to punish them on the east. He gave tranquillity to their people, who welcomed him with baskets full of their black and yellow silks, saying– "From henceforth we shall serve the sovereign of our dynasty of Châu, that we may be made happy by him." So they joined themselves, as subjects, to the great city of Châu. Thus, the men of station of Shang took baskets full of black and yellow silks to meet the men of station of Châu, and the lower classes of the one met those of the other with baskets of rice and vessels of congee. Wû saved the people from the midst of fire and water, seizing only their oppressors, and destroying them.'

6. 'In the Great Declaration it is said, "My power shall be put forth, and, invading the territories of Shang, I will seize the oppressor. I will put him to death to punish him:– so shall the greatness of my work appear, more glorious than that of T'ang."

7. 'Sung is not, as you say, practising true royal government, and so forth. If it were practising royal government, all within the four seas would be lifting up their heads, and looking for its prince, wishing to have him for their sovereign. Great as Ch'î and Ch'û are, what would there be to fear from them?'

CHAPTER 12

1. Mencius said to Tâi Pû-shang, 'I see that you are desiring your king to be virtuous, and will plainly tell you how he may be made so. Suppose that there is a great officer of Ch'û here, who wishes his son to learn the speech of Ch'î. Will he in that case employ a man of Ch'î as his tutor, or a man of Ch'û?' 'He will employ a man of Ch'î to teach him.' said Pû-shang. Mencius went on, 'If but one man of Ch'î be teaching him, and there be a multitude of men of Ch'û continually shouting out about him, although his father beat him every day, wishing him to learn the speech of Ch'î, it will be impossible for him to do so. But in the same way, if he were to be taken and placed for several years in Chwang or Yo, though his father should beat him, wishing him to speak the language of Ch'û, it would be impossible for him to do so.

2. 'You supposed that Hsieh Chü-châu was a scholar of virtue, and you have got him placed in attendance on the king. Suppose that all in attendance on the king, old and young, high and low, were Hsieh Chü-châus, whom would the king have to do evil with? And suppose that all in attendance on the king, old and young, high and low, are not Hsieh Chü-châus, whom will the king have to do good with? What can one Hsieh Chü-châu do alone for the king of Sung?'

•

1. Kung-sun Châu asked Mencius, saying, 'What is the point of righteousness involved in your not going to see the princes?' Mencius replied, 'Among the ancients, if one had not been a minister in a State, he did not go to see the sovereign.

2. 'Twan Kan-mû leaped over his wall to avoid the prince. Hsieh Liû shut his door, and would not admit the prince. These two, however, carried their scrupulosity to excess. When a prince is urgent, it is not improper to see him.

3. 'Yang Ho wished to get Confucius to go to see him, but disliked doing so by any want of propriety. As it is the rule, therefore, that when a great officer sends a gift to a scholar, if the latter be not at home to receive it, he must go to the officer's to pay his respects, Yang Ho watched when Confucius was out, and sent him a roasted pig. Confucius, in his turn, watched when Ho was out, and went to pay his respects to him. At that time, Yang Ho had taken the initiative;– how could Confucius decline going to see him?

4. 'Tsang-tsze said, "They who shrug up their shoulders, and laugh in a flattering way, toil harder than the summer labourer in the fields." Tsze-lû said, "There are those who talk with people with whom they have no great community of feeling. If you look at their countenances, they are full of blushes. I do not

desire to know such persons." By considering these remarks, the spirit which the superior man nourishes may be known.'

•

1. Tâi Ying-chih said to Mencius, 'I am not able at present and immediately to do with the levying of a tithe only, and abolishing the duties charged at the passes and in the markets. With your leave I will lighten, however, both the tax and the duties, until next year, and will then make an end of them. What do you think of such a course?'

2. Mencius said, 'Here is a man, who every day appropriates some of his neighbour's strayed fowls. Some one says to him, "Such is not the way of a good man;" and he replies, "With your leave I will diminish my appropriations, and will take only one fowl a month, until next year, when I will make an end of the practice."

3. 'If you know that the thing is unrighteous, then use all despatch in putting an end to it:– why wait till next year?'

•

1. The disciple Kung-tû said to Mencius, 'Master, the people beyond our school all speak of you as being fond of disputing. I venture to ask whether it be so.' Mencius replied, 'Indeed, I am not fond of disputing, but I am compelled to do it.

2. 'A long time has elapsed since this world of men received its being, and there has been along its history now a period of good order, and now a period of confusion.

3. 'In the time of Yâo, the waters, flowing out of their channels, inundated the Middle Kingdom. Snakes and dragons occupied it, and the people had no place where they could settle themselves. In the low grounds they made nests for themselves on the trees or raised platforms, and in the high grounds they made caves. It is said in the Book of History, "The waters in their wild course warned me." Those "waters in their wild course" were the waters of the great inundation.

4. 'Shun employed Yü to reduce the waters to order. Yü dug open their obstructed channels, and conducted them to the sea. He drove away the snakes and dragons, and forced them into the grassy marshes. On this, the waters pursued their course through the country, even the waters of the Chiang, the Hwâi, the Ho, and the Han, and the dangers and obstructions which they had occasioned were removed. The birds and beasts which had injured the people also disappeared, and after this men found the plains available for them, and occupied them.

5. 'After the death of Yâo and Shun, the principles that mark sages fell into decay. Oppressive sovereigns arose one after another, who pulled down houses to make ponds and lakes, so that the people knew not where they could rest in quiet; they threw fields out of cultivation to form gardens and parks, so that the people could not get clothes and food. Afterwards, corrupt speakings and oppressive deeds became more rife; gardens and parks, ponds and lakes, thickets and marshes became more numerous, and birds and beasts swarmed. By the time of the tyrant Châu, the kingdom was again in a state of great confusion.

6. 'Châu-kung assisted king Wû, and destroyed Châu. He smote Yen, and after three years put its sovereign to death. He drove Fei-lien to a corner by the sea, and slew him. The States which he extinguished amounted to fifty. He drove far away also the tigers, leopards, rhinoceroses, and elephants;– and all the people was greatly delighted. It is said in the Book of History, "Great and splendid were the plans of king Wan! Greatly were they carried out by the energy of king Wû! They are for the assistance and instruction of us who are of an after day. They are all in principle correct, and deficient in nothing."

7. 'Again the world fell into decay, and principles faded away. Perverse speakings and oppressive deeds waxed rife again. There were instances of ministers who murdered their sovereigns, and of sons who murdered their fathers

8. 'Confucius was afraid, and made the "Spring and Autumn." What the "Spring and Autumn" contains are matters proper to the sovereign. On this account Confucius said, "Yes! It is the Spring and Autumn which will make men know me, and it is the Spring and Autumn which will make men condemn me."

9. 'Once more, sage sovereigns cease to arise, and the princes of the States give the reins to their lusts. Unemployed scholars indulge in unreasonable discussions. The words of Yang Chû and Mo Tî fill the country. If you listen to people's discourses throughout it, you will find that they have adopted the views either of Yang or of Mo. Now, Yang's principle is– "each one for himself," which does not acknowledge the claims of the sovereign. Mo's principle is– "to love all equally," which does not acknowledge the peculiar affection due to a father. But to acknowledge neither king nor father is to be in the state of a beast. Kung-ming Î said, "In their kitchens, there is fat meat. In their stables, there are fat horses. But their people have the look of hunger, and on the wilds there are those who have died of famine. This is leading on beasts to devour men." If the principles of Yang and Mo be not stopped, and the principles of Confucius not set forth, then those perverse speakings will delude the people, and stop up the path of benevolence and righteousness. When benevolence and righteousness are stopped up, beasts will be led on to devour men, and men will devour one another.

10. 'I am alarmed by these things, and address myself to the defence of the doctrines of the former sages, and to oppose Yang and Mo. I drive away their licentious expressions, so that such perverse speakers may not be able to show themselves. Their delusions spring up in men's minds, and do injury to their practice of affairs. Shown in their practice of affairs, they are pernicious to their government. When sages shall rise up again, they will not change my words.

11. 'In former times, Yü repressed the vast waters of the inundation, and the country was reduced to order. Châu-kung's achievements extended even to the barbarous tribes of the east and north, and he drove away all ferocious animals, and the people enjoyed repose. Confucius completed the "Spring and Autumn," and rebellious ministers and villainous sons were struck with terror.

12. 'It is said in the Book of Poetry,

> *He smote the barbarians of the west and the north;*
> *He punished Ching and Shû*
> *And no one dared to resist us.*

These father-deniers and king-deniers would have been smitten by Châu-kung.

13. 'I also wish to rectify men's hearts, and to put an end to those perverse doctrines, to oppose their one-sided actions and banish away their licentious expressions;– and thus to carry on the work of the three sages. Do I do so because I am fond of disputing? I am compelled to do it.

14. 'Whoever is able to oppose Yang and Mo is a disciple of the sages.'

•

1. K'wang Chang said to Mencius, 'Is not Ch'an Chung a man of true self-denying purity? He was living in Wû-ling, and for three days was without food, till he could neither hear nor see. Over a well there grew a plum-tree, the fruit of which had been more than half eaten by worms. He crawled to it, and tried to eat some of the fruit, when, after swallowing three mouthfuls, he recovered his sight and hearing.'

2. Mencius replied, 'Among the scholars of Ch'î, I must regard Chung as the thumb among the fingers. But still, where is the self-denying purity he pretends to? To carry out the principles which he holds, one must become an earthworm, for so only can it be done.

3. 'Now, an earthworm eats the dry mould above, and drinks the yellow spring below. Was the house in which Chung dwells built by a Po-î? or was it built by a robber like Chih? Was the millet which he eats planted by a Po-î? or was it planted by a robber like Chih? These are things which cannot be known.'

4. 'But,' said Chang, 'what does that matter? He himself weaves sandals of hemp, and his wife twists and dresses threads of hemp to sell or exchange them.'

5. Mencius rejoined, 'Chung belongs to an ancient and noble family of Ch'î. His elder brother Tâi received from Kâ a revenue of 10,000 chung, but he considered his brother's emolument to be unrighteous, and would not eat of it, and in the same way he considered his brother's house to be unrighteous, and would not dwell in it. Avoiding his brother and leaving his mother, he went and dwelt in Wû-ling. One day afterwards, he returned to their house, when it happened that some one sent his brother a present of a live goose. He, knitting his eyebrows, said, "What are you going to use that cackling thing for?" By-and-by his mother killed the goose, and gave him some of it to eat. Just then his brother came into the house, and said, "It is the flesh of that cackling thing," upon which he went out and vomited it.

6. 'Thus, what his mother gave him he would not eat, but what his wife gives him he eats. He will not dwell in his brother's house, but he dwells in Wû-ling. How can he in such circumstances complete the style of life which he professes? With such principles as Chung holds, a man must be an earthworm, and then he can carry them out.'

CHAPTER 13

1. Mencius said, 'The power of vision of Lî Lâu, and skill of hand of Kung-shû, without the compass and square, could not form squares and circles. The acute ear of the music-master K'wang, without the pitch-tubes, could not determine correctly the five notes. The principles of Yâo and Shun, without a benevolent government, could not secure the tranquil order of the kingdom.

2. 'There are now princes who have benevolent hearts and a reputation for benevolence, while yet the people do not receive any benefits from them, nor will they leave any example to future ages;– all because they do not put into practice the ways of the ancient kings.

3. 'Hence we have the saying:– "Virtue alone is not sufficient for the exercise of government; laws alone cannot carry themselves into practice."

4. It is said in the Book of Poetry,

> *Without transgression, without forgetfulness,*
> *Following the ancient statutes.*

Never has any one fallen into error, who followed the laws of the ancient kings.

5. 'When the sages had used the vigour of their eyes, they called in to their aid the compass, the square, the level, and the line, to make things square, round, level, and straight:– the use of the instruments is inexhaustible. When they had used their power of hearing to the utmost, they called in the pitch-tubes to their aid to determine the five notes:– the use of those tubes is inexhaustible. When they had exerted to the utmost the thoughts of their hearts, they called in to their aid a government that could not endure to witness the sufferings of men:– and their benevolence overspread the kingdom.

6. 'Hence we have the saying:– "To raise a thing high, we must begin from the top of a mound or a hill; to dig to a great depth, we must commence in the low ground of a stream or a marsh." Can he be pronounced wise, who, in the exercise of government, does not proceed according to the ways of the former kings?

7. 'Therefore only the benevolent ought to be in high stations. When a man destitute of benevolence is in a high station, he thereby disseminates his wickedness among all below him.

8. 'When the prince has no principles by which he examines his administration, and his ministers have no laws by which they keep themselves in the discharge

of their duties, then in the court obedience is not paid to principle, and in the office obedience is not paid to rule. Superiors violate the laws of righteousness, and inferiors violate the penal laws. It is only by a fortunate chance that a State in such a case is preserved.

9. 'Therefore it is said, "It is not the exterior and interior walls being incomplete, and the supply of weapons offensive and defensive not being large, which constitutes the calamity of a kingdom. It is not the cultivable area not being extended, and stores and wealth not being accumulated, which occasions the ruin of a State." When superiors do not observe the rules of propriety, and inferiors do not learn, then seditious people spring up, and that State will perish in no time.

10. 'It is said in the Book of Poetry,

When such an overthrow of Châu is being produced by Heaven,
Be not ye so much at your ease!

11. ' "At your ease;"– that is, dilatory.

12. 'And so dilatory may those officers be deemed, who serve their prince without righteousness, who take office and retire from it without regard to propriety, and who in their words disown the ways of the ancient kings.

13. 'Therefore it is said, "To urge one's sovereign to difficult achievements may be called showing respect for him. To set before him what is good and repress his perversities may be called showing reverence for him. He who does not do these things, saying to himself,– My sovereign is incompetent to this, may be said to play the thief with him." '

•

1. Mencius said, 'The compass and square produce perfect circles and squares. By the sages, the human relations are perfectly exhibited.

2. 'He who as a sovereign would perfectly discharge the duties of a sovereign, and he who as a minister would perfectly discharge the duties of a minister, have only to imitate– the one Yâo, and the other Shun. He who does not serve his sovereign as Shun served Yâo, does not respect his sovereign; and he who does not rule his people as Yâo ruled his, injures his people.

3. 'Confucius said, "There are but two courses, which can be pursued, that of virtue and its opposite."

4. 'A ruler who carries the oppression of his people to the highest pitch, will himself be slain, and his kingdom will perish. If one stop short of the highest pitch, his life will notwithstanding be in danger, and his kingdom will be weakened. He will be styled "The Dark," or "The Cruel," and though he may

have filial sons and affectionate grandsons, they will not be able in a hundred generations to change the designation.

5. 'This is what is intended in the words of the Book of Poetry,

The beacon of Yin is not remote,
It is in the time of the (last) sovereign of Hsiâ.'

•

1. Mencius said, 'It was by benevolence that the three dynasties gained the throne, and by not being benevolent that they lost it.

2. 'It is by the same means that the decaying and flourishing, the preservation and perishing, of States are determined.

3. 'If the sovereign be not benevolent, be cannot preserve the throne from passing from him. If the Head of a State be not benevolent, he cannot preserve his rule. If a high noble or great officer be not benevolent, he cannot preserve his ancestral temple. If a scholar or common man be not benevolent, be cannot preserve his four limbs

4. 'Now they hate death and ruin, and yet delight in being not benevolent;– this is like hating to be drunk, and yet being strong to drink wine!

•

1. Mencius said, 'If a man love others, and no responsive attachment is shown to him, let him turn inwards and examine his own benevolence. If he is trying to rule others, and his government is unsuccessful, let him turn inwards and examine his wisdom. If he treats others politely, and they do not return his politeness, let him turn inwards and examine his own feeling of respect.

2. 'When we do not, by what we do, realise what we desire, we must turn inwards, and examine ourselves in every point. When a man's person is correct, the whole kingdom will turn to him with recognition and submission.

3. 'It is said in the Book of Poetry,

Be always studious to be in harmony with the ordinances of God,
And you will obtain much happiness.'

•

Mencius said, 'People have this common saying,– "The kingdom, the State, the family." The root of the kingdom is in the State. The root of the State is in the family. The root of the family is in the person of its Head.'

•

Mencius said, 'The administration of government is not difficult;– it lies in not offending the great families. He whom the great families affect, will be affected by the whole State; and he whom any one State affects, will be affected by the whole kingdom. When this is the case, such an one's virtue and teachings will spread over all within the four seas like the rush of water.'

•

1. Mencius said, 'When right government prevails in the kingdom, princes of little virtue are submissive to those of great, and those of little worth to those of great. When bad government prevails in the kingdom, princes of small power are submissive to those of great, and the weak to the strong. Both these cases are the rule of Heaven. They who accord with Heaven are preserved, and they who rebel against Heaven perish.

2. 'The duke Ching of Ch'î said, "Not to be able to command others, and at the same time to refuse to receive their commands, is to cut one's self off from all intercourse with others." His tears flowed forth while he gave his daughter to be married to the prince of Wû.

3. 'Now the small States imitate the large, and yet are ashamed to receive their commands. This is like a scholar's being ashamed to receive the commands of his master.

4. 'For a prince who is ashamed of this, the best plan is to imitate king Wan. Let one imitate king Wan, and in five years, if his State be large, or in seven years, if it be small, he will be sure to give laws to the kingdom.

5. 'It is said in the Book of Poetry,

> The descendants of the sovereigns of the Shang dynasty,
> Are in number more than hundreds of thousands,
> But, God having passed His decree,
> They are all submissive to Châu.
> They are submissive to Châu,
> Because the decree of Heaven is not unchanging.
> The officers of Yin, admirable and alert,
> Pour out the libations, and assist in the capital of Châu.

Confucius said, "As against so benevolent a sovereign, they could not be deemed a multitude." Thus, if the prince of a state love benevolence, he will have no opponent in all the kingdom.

6. 'Now they wish to have no opponent in all the kingdom, but they do not seek to attain this by being benevolent. This is like a man laying hold of a heated substance, and not having first dipped it in water. It is said in the Book of Poetry,

> Who can take up a heated substance,
> Without first dipping it (in water)?'

•

1. Mencius said, 'How is it possible to speak with those princes who are not benevolent ? Their perils they count safety, their calamities they count profitable, and they have pleasure in the things by which they perish. If it were possible to talk with them who so violate benevolence, how could we have such destruction of States and ruin of Families?

2. 'There was a boy singing,
When the water of the Ts'ang-lang is clear,
It does to wash the strings of my cap;
When the water of the Ts'ang-lang is muddy,
It does to wash my feet.

3. 'Confucius said, "Hear what he sings, my children. When clear, then he will wash his cap-strings; and when muddy, he will wash his feet with it. This different application is brought by the water on itself."

4. 'A man must first despise himself, and then others will despise him. A family must first destroy itself, and then others will destroy it. A State must first smite itself, and then others will smite it.

5. 'This is illustrated in the passage of the T'âi Chiâ, "When Heaven sends down calamities, it is still possible to escape them. When we occasion the calamities ourselves, it is not possible any longer to live."'

•

1. Mencius said, 'Chieh and Châu's losing the empire, arose from their losing the people, and to lose the people means to lose their hearts. There is a way to get the kingdom:– get the people, and the kingdom is got. There is a way to get the people:– get their hearts, and the people are got. There is a way to get their hearts:– it is simply to collect for them what they like, and not to lay on them what they dislike.

2. 'The people turn to a benevolent rule as water flows downwards, and as wild beasts fly to the wilderness.

3. 'Accordingly, as the otter aids the deep waters, driving the fish into them, and the hawk aids the thickets, driving the little birds to them, so Chieh and Châu aided T'ang and Wû, driving the people to them.

4. 'If among the present rulers of the kingdom, there were one who loved benevolence, all the other princes would aid him, by driving the people to him. Although he wished not to become sovereign, he could not avoid becoming so.

5. 'The case of one of the present princes wishing to become sovereign is like

the having to seek for mugwort three years old, to cure a seven years' sickness. If it have not been kept in store, the patient may all his life not get it. If the princes do not set their wills on benevolence, all their days will be in sorrow and disgrace, and they will be involved in death and ruin.

6. 'This is illustrated by what is said in the Book of Poetry,

> *How otherwise can you improve the kingdom?*
> *You will only with it go to ruin.'*

•

1. Mencius said, 'With those who do violence to themselves, it is impossible to speak. With those who throw themselves away, it is impossible to do anything. To disown in his conversation propriety and righteousness, is what we mean by doing violence to one's self. To say– "I am not able to dwell in benevolence or pursue the path of righteousness," is what we mean by throwing one's self away.

2. 'Benevolence is the tranquil habitation of man, and righteousness is his straight path.

3. 'Alas for them, who leave the tranquil dwelling empty and do not reside in it, and who abandon the right path and do not pursue it!'

CHAPTER 14

Mencius said, 'The path of duty lies in what is near, and men seek for it in what is remote. The work of duty lies in what is easy, and men seek for it in what is difficult. If each man would love his parents and show the due respect to his elders, the whole land would enjoy tranquillity.'

•

1. Mencius said, 'When those occupying inferior situations do not obtain the confidence of the sovereign, they cannot succeed in governing the people. There is a way to obtain the confidence of the sovereign:– if one is not trusted by his friends, he will not obtain the confidence of his sovereign. There is a way of being trusted by one's friends:– if one do not serve his parents so as to make them pleased, he will not be trusted by his friends. There is a way to make one's parents pleased:– if one, on turning his thoughts inwards, finds a want of sincerity, he will not give pleasure to his parents. There is a way to the attainment of sincerity in one's self:– if a man do not understand what is good, he will not attain sincerity in himself.

2. 'Therefore, sincerity is the way of Heaven. To think how to be sincere is the way of man.

3. Never has there been one possessed of complete sincerity, who did not move others. Never has there been one who had not sincerity who was able to move others.'

•

1. Mencius said, 'Po-Î, that he might avoid Châ'u, was dwelling on the coast of the northern sea. When he heard of the rise of king Wan, he roused himself, and said, "Why should I not go and follow him? I have heard that the chief of the West knows well how to nourish the old." T'âi-kung, that he might avoid Châu, was dwelling on the coast of the eastern sea. When he heard of the rise of king Wan, he roused himself, and said, "Why should I not go and follow him? I have heard that the chief of the West knows well how to nourish the old."

2. 'Those two old men were the greatest old men of the kingdom. When they came to follow king Wan, it was the fathers of the kingdom coming to follow him. When the fathers of the kingdom joined him, how could the sons go to any other?

3. 'Were any of the princes to practise the government of king Wan, within seven years he would be sure to be giving laws to the kingdom.'

•

1. Mencius said, 'Ch'iû acted as chief officer to the head of the Chî family, whose evil ways he was unable to change, while he exacted from the people double the grain formerly paid. Confucius said, "He is no disciple of mine. Little children, beat the drum and assail him."

2. 'Looking at the subject from this case, we perceive that when a prince was not practising benevolent government, all his ministers who enriched him were rejected by Confucius:– how much more would he have rejected those who are vehement to fight for their prince! When contentions about territory are the ground on which they fight, they slaughter men till the fields are filled with them. When some struggle for a city is the ground on which they fight, they slaughter men till the city is filled with them. This is what is called "leading on the land to devour human flesh." Death is not enough for such a crime.

3. 'Therefore, those who are skilful to fight should suffer the highest punishment. Next to them should be punished those who unite some princes in leagues against others; and next to them, those who take in grassy commons, imposing the cultivation of the ground on the people.'

•

1. Mencius said, "Of all the parts of a man's body there is none more excellent than the pupil of the eye. The pupil cannot be used to hide a man's wickedness. If within the breast all be correct, the pupil is bright. If within the breast all be not correct, the pupil is dull.

2. 'Listen to a man's words and look at the pupil of his eye. How can a man conceal his character?'

Mencius said, 'The respectful do not despise others. The economical do not plunder others. The prince who treats men with despite and plunders them, is only afraid that they may not prove obedient to him:– how can he be regarded as respectful or economical? How can respectfulness and economy be made out of tones of the voice, and a smiling manner?'

•

1. Shun-yü K'wan said, 'Is it the rule that males and females shall not allow their hands to touch in giving or receiving anything?' Mencius replied, 'It is the rule.' K'wan asked, 'If a man's sister-in-law be drowning, shall he rescue her with his hand?' Mencius said, 'He who would not so rescue the drowning woman is a wolf. For males and females not to allow their hands to touch in giving and receiving is the general rule; when a sister-in-law is drowning, to rescue her with the hand is a peculiar exigency.'

2. K'wan said, 'The whole kingdom is drowning. How strange it is that you will not rescue it!'

3. Mencius answered, 'A drowning kingdom must be rescued with right principles, as a drowning sister-in-law has to be rescued with the hand. Do you wish me to rescue the kingdom with my hand?'

•

1. Kung-sun Chow said, "Why is it that the superior man does not himself teach his son?"

2. Mencius replied, 'The circumstances of the case forbid its being done. The teacher must inculcate what is correct. When he inculcates what is correct, and his lessons are not practised, he follows them up with being angry. When he follows them up with being angry, then, contrary to what should be, he is offended with his son. At the same time, the pupil says, 'My master inculcates on me what is correct, and he himself does not proceed in a correct path." The result of this is, that father and son are offended with each other. When father and son come to be offended with each other, the case is evil.

3. 'The ancients exchanged sons, and one taught the son of another.

4. 'Between father and son, there should be no reproving admonitions to what is good. Such reproofs lead to alienation, and than alienation there is nothing more inauspicious.'

•

1. Mencius said, 'Of services, which is the greatest? The service of parents is the greatest. Of charges, which is the greatest ? The charge of one's self is the greatest. That those who do not fail to keep themselves are able to serve their parents is what I have heard. But I have never heard of any, who, having failed to keep themselves, were able notwithstanding to serve their parents.

2. 'There are many services, but the service of parents is the root of all others. There are many charges, but the charge of one's self is the root of all others.

3. 'The philosopher Tsang, in nourishing Tsang Hsî, was always sure to have wine and flesh provided. And when they were being removed, he would ask respectfully to whom he should give what was left. If his father asked whether there was anything left, he was sure to say, "There is." After the death of Tsang Hsî, when Tsang Yüan came to nourish the philosopher Tsang, he was always sure to have wine and flesh provided. But when the things were being removed, he did not ask to whom he should give what was left, and if his father asked whether there was anything left, he would answer "No;"– intending to bring them in again. This was what is called– "nourishing the mouth and body." We may call the philosopher Tsang's practice– "nourishing the will."

4. 'To serve one's parents as the philosopher Tsang served his, may be accepted as flial piety.'

•

Mencius said, 'It is not enough to remonstrate with a sovereign on account of the mal-employment of ministers, nor to blame errors of government. It is only the great man who can rectify what is wrong in the sovereign's mind. Let the prince be benevolent, and all his acts will be benevolent. Let the prince be righteous, and all his acts will be righteous. Let the prince be correct, and everything will be correct. Once rectify the ruler, and the kingdom will be firmly settled.'

•

Mencius said, 'There are cases of praise which could not be expected, and of reproach when the parties have been seeking to be perfect.'

•

Mencius said, 'Men's being ready with their tongues arises simply from their not having been reproved'.

•

Mencius said, "The evil of men is that they like to be teachers of others'.

•

1. The disciple Yo-chang went in the train of Tsze-âo to Ch'î.

2. He came to see Mencius, who said to him, 'Are you also come to see me?' Yo-chang replied, 'Master, why do you speak such words?' 'How many days have you been here?' asked Mencius. 'I came yesterday.' 'Yesterday! Is it not with reason then that I thus speak?' 'My lodging-house was not arranged.' 'Have you heard that a scholar's lodging-house must be arranged before he visit his elder?'

3. Yo-chang said, 'I have done wrong.'

Mencius, addressing the disciple Yo-chang, said to him, 'Your coming here in the train of Tsze-âo was only because of the food and the drink. I could not have thought that you, having learned the doctrine of the ancients, would have acted with a view to eating and drinking.'

•

1. Mencius said, 'There are three things which are unfilial, and to have no posterity is the greatest of them.

2. 'Shun married without informing his parents because of this,– lest he should have no posterity. Superior men consider that his doing so was the same as if he had informed them.'

•

1. Mencius said, 'The richest fruit of benevolence is this – the service of one's parents. The richest fruit of righteousness is this – the obeying one's elder brothers.

2. 'The richest fruit of wisdom is this,– the knowing those two things, and not departing from them. The richest fruit of propriety is this,– the ordering and adorning those two things. The richest fruit of music is this,– the rejoicing in those two things. When they are rejoiced in, they grow. Growing, how can they be repressed? When they come to this state that they cannot be repressed, then unconsciously the feet begin to dance and the hands to move.'

•

1. Mencius said, "Suppose the case of the whole empire turning in great delight to an individual to submit to him. – To regard the whole empire thus turning to him in great delight as but a bundle of grass – only Shun was capable of this. He considered that if one could not get the hearts of his parents he could not be considered a man, and that if he could not get an entire accord with his parents, he could not be considered a son'.

2. 'By Shun's completely fulfilling everything by which a parent could be served, Kû-sâu was brought to find delight in what was good. When Kû-sâu was brought to find that delight, the whole kingdom was transformed. When Kû-sâu was brought to find that delight, all fathers and sons in the kingdom were established in their respective duties. This is called great filial piety.'

CHAPTER 15

1. Mencius said, 'Shun was born in Chû-fang, removed to Fû-hsiâ, and died in Ming-t'iâo;– a man near the wild tribes on the east.

2. 'King Wan was born in Châu by mount Ch'î, and died in Pî-ying;– a man near the wild tribes on the west.

3. 'Those regions were distant from one another more than a thousand lî, and the age of the one sage was posterior to that of the other more than a thousand years. But when they got their wish, and carried their principles into practice throughout the Middle Kingdom, it was like uniting the two halves of a seal.

4. 'When we examine those sages, both the earlier and the later, their principles are found to be the same.'

●

1. When Tsze-ch'an was chief minister of the State of Chang, he would convey people across the Chan and Wei in his own carriage.

2. Mencius said, 'It was kind, but showed that he did not understand the practice of government.

3. 'When in the eleventh month of the year the foot-bridges are completed, and the carriage-bridges in the twelfth month, the people have not the trouble of wading.

4. 'Let a governor conduct his rule on principles of equal justice, and, when he goes abroad, he may cause people to be removed out of his path. But how can he convey everybody across the rivers?

5. 'It follows that if a governor will try to please everybody, he will find the days not sufficient for his work.'

●

1. Mencius said to the king Hsüan of Ch'î, 'When the prince regards his ministers as his hands and feet, his ministers regard their prince as their belly and heart; when he regards them as his dogs and horses, they regard him as another man; when he regards them as the ground or as grass, they regard him as a robber and an enemy.'

2. The king said, 'According to the rules of propriety, a minister wears mourning when he has left the service of a prince. How must a prince behave that his old ministers may thus go into mourning?'

3. Mencius replied,'The admonitions of a minister having been followed, and

his advice listened to, so that blessings have descended on the people, if for some cause he leaves the country, the prince sends an escort to conduct him beyond the boundaries. He also anticipates with recommendatory intimations his arrival in the country to which he is proceeding. When he has been gone three years and does not return, only then at length does he take back his fields and residence. This treatment is what is called a "thrice-repeated display of consideration." When a prince acts thus, mourning will be worn on leaving his service.

4. 'Nowadays, the remonstrances of a minister are not followed, and his advice is not listened to, so that no blessings descend on the people. When for any cause he leaves the country, the prince tries to seize him and hold him a prisoner. He also pushes him to extremity in the country to which he has gone, and on the very day of his departure, takes back his fields and residence. This treatment shows him to be what we call "a robber and an enemy." What mourning can be worn for a robber and an enemy?'

•

Mencius said, 'When scholars are put to death without any crime, the great officers may leave the country. When the people are slaughtered without any crime, the scholars may remove.'

Mencius said, 'If the sovereign be benevolent, all will be benevolent. If the sovereign be righteous, all will be righteous.'

Mencius said, 'Acts of propriety which are not really proper, and acts of righteousness which are not really righteous, the great man does not do.'

Mencius said, 'Those who keep the Mean, train up those who do not, and those who have abilities, train up those who have not, and hence men rejoice in having fathers and elder brothers who are possessed of virtue and talent. If they who keep the Mean spurn those who do not, and they who have abilities spurn those who have not, then the space between them– those so gifted and the ungifted– will not admit an inch.'

•

Mencius said, 'Men must be decided on what they will NOT do, and then they are able to act with vigour in what they ought to do.'

Mencius said, 'What future misery have they and ought they to endure, who talk of what is not good in others!'

Mencius said, 'Chung-ne did not do extraordinary things.'

Mencius said,'The great man does not think beforehand of his words that they may be sincere, nor of his actions that they may be resolute;– he simply speaks and does what is right.'

•

Mencius said, 'The great man is he who does not lose his child's-heart.'

•

Mencius said, 'The nourishment of parents when living is not sufficient to be accounted the great thing. It is only in performing their obsequies when dead, that we have what can be considered the great thing.'

•

Mencius said, 'The superior man makes his advances in what he is learning with deep earnestness and by the proper course, wishing to get hold of it as in himself. Having got hold of it in himself, he abides in it calmly and firmly. Abiding in it calmly and firmly, he reposes a deep reliance on it. Reposing a deep reliance on it, he seizes it on the left and right, meeting everywhere with it as a fountain from which things flow. It is on this account that the superior man wishes to get hold of what he is learning as in himself.'

•

Mencius said, 'In learning extensively and discussing minutely what is learned, the object of the superior man is that he may be able to go back and set forth in brief what is essential.'

•

Mencius said, 'Never has he who would by his excellence subdue men been able to subdue them. Let a prince seek by his excellence to nourish men, and he will be able to subdue the whole empire. It is impossible that anyone should become ruler of the empire to whom it has not yielded the subjection of the heart.'

•

Mencius said, 'Words which are not true are inauspicious, and the words which are most truly obnoxious to the name of inauspicious, are those which throw into the shade men of talents and virtue.'

•

1. The disciple Hsü said, 'Chung-nî often praised water, saying, "O water! O water!" What did he find in water to praise?'

2. Mencius replied, 'There is a spring of water; how it gushes out! It rests not day nor night. It fills up every hole, and then advances, flowing onto the four seas. Such is water having a spring! It was this which he found in it to praise.

3. 'But suppose that the water has no spring.– In the seventh and eighth months when the rain falls abundantly, the channels in the fields are all filled, but

their being dried up again may be expected in a short time. So a superior man is ashamed of a reputation beyond his merits.'

•

1. Mencius said, 'That whereby man differs from the lower animals is but small. The mass of people cast it away, while superior men preserve it.

2. 'Shun clearly understood the multitude of things, and closely observed the relations of humanity. He walked along the path of benevolence and righteousness; he did not need to pursue benevolence and righteousness.'

•

1. Mencius said, 'Yü hated the pleasant wine, and loved good words.

2. 'T'ang held fast the Mean, and employed men of talents and virtue without regard to where they came from.

3. 'King Wan looked on the people as he would on a man who was wounded, and he looked towards the right path as if he could not see it.

4. King Wû did not slight the near, and did not forget the distant.

5. 'The duke of Châu desired to unite in himself the virtues of those kings, those founders of the three dynasties, that he might display in his practice the four things which they did. If he saw any thing in them not suited to his time, he looked up and thought about it, from daytime into the night, and when he was fortunate enough to master the difficulty, he sat waiting for the morning.'

•

1. Mencius said, 'The traces of imperial rule were extinguished, and the imperial odes ceased to be made. When those odes ceased to be made, then the 'Ch'un Ch'iû' was produced.

2. 'The 'Shang' of Tsin, the 'Tâo-wû' of Ch'û, and the 'Ch'un Ch'iû' of Lû were books of the same character.

3. 'The subject of the Ch'un Ch'iû was the affairs of Hwan of Chî and Wan of Tsin, and its style was the historical. Confucius said, "Its righteous decisions I ventured to make."'

•

1. Mencius said, 'The influence of a sovereign sage terminates in the fifth generation. The influence of a mere sage does the same.

2. 'Although I could not be a disciple of Confucius himself, I have endeavoured to cultivate my virtue by means of others who were.'

CHAPTER 16

Mencius said, 'When it appears proper to take a thing, and afterwards not proper, to take it is contrary to moderation. When it appears proper to give a thing and afterwards not proper, to give it is contrary to kindness. When it appears proper to sacrifice one's life, and afterwards not proper, to sacrifice it is contrary to bravery.'

•

1. P'ang Mang learned archery of Î. When he had acquired completely all the science of Î, he thought that in all the kingdom only Î was superior to himself, and so he slew him. Mencius said, 'In this case Î also was to blame. Kung-ming Î indeed said, "It would appear as if he were not to be blamed," but he thereby only meant that his blame was slight. How can he be held without any blame?'

2. 'The people of Chang sent Tsze-cho Yü to make a stealthy attack on Wei, which sent Yü-kung Sze to pursue him. Tsze-cho Yü said, "To-day I feel unwell, so that I cannot hold my bow. I am a dead man!" At the same time he asked his driver, "Who is it that is pursuing me?" The driver said, "It is Yü-kung Sze," on which, he exclaimed, "I shall live." The driver said, "Yü-kung Sze is the best archer of Wei, what do you mean by saying 'I shall live?'" Yü replied, "Yü-kung Sze learned archery from Yin-kung T'o, who again learned it from me. Now, Yin-kung T'o is an upright man, and the friends of his selection must be upright also." When Yü-kung Sze came up, he said, "Master, why are you not holding your bow?" Yü answered him, "To-day I am feeling unwell, and cannot hold my bow." On this Sze said, "I learned archery from Yin-kung T'o, who again learned it from you. I cannot bear to injure you with your own science. The business of to-day, however, is the prince's business, which I dare not neglect." He then took his arrows, knocked off their steel points against the carriage-wheel, discharged four of them, and returned.

•

1. Mencius said, 'If the lady Hsî had been covered with a filthy head-dress, all people would have stopped their noses in passing her.

2. 'Though a man may be wicked, yet if he adjust his thoughts, fast, and bathe, he may sacrifice to God.'

•

1. Mencius said, 'All who speak about the natures of things, have in fact only their phenomena to reason from, and the value of a phenomenon is in its being natural.

2. 'What I dislike in your wise men is their boring out their conclusions. If those wise men would only act as Yü did when he conveyed away the waters, there would be nothing to dislike in their wisdom. The manner in which Yü conveyed away the waters was by doing what gave him no trouble. If your wise men would also do that which gave them no trouble, their knowledge would also be great.

3. 'There is heaven so high; there are the stars so distant. If we have investigated their phenomena, we may, while sitting in our places, go back to the solstice of a thousand years ago.'

•

1. The officer Kung-hang having on hand the funeral of one of his sons, the Master of the Right went to condole with him. When this noble entered the door, some called him to them and spoke with him, and some went to his place and spoke with him.

2. Mencius did not speak with him, so that he was displeased, and said, 'All the gentlemen have spoken with me. There is only Mencius who does not speak to me, thereby slighting me.'

3. Mencius having heard of this remark, said, 'According to the prescribed rules, in the court, individuals may not change their places to speak with one another, nor may they pass from their ranks to bow to one another. I was wishing to observe this rule, and Tsze-âo understands it that I was slighting him:– is not this strange?'

•

1. Mencius said, 'That whereby the superior man is distinguished from other men is what he preserves in his heart;– namely, benevolence and propriety.

2. 'The benevolent man loves others. The man of propriety shows respect to others.

3. 'He who loves others is constantly loved by them. He who respects others is constantly respected by them.

4. 'Here is a man, who treats me in a perverse and unreasonable manner. The superior man in such a case will turn round upon himself– "I must have been wanting in benevolence; I must have been wanting in propriety;– how should this have happened to me?"

5. He examines himself, and is specially benevolent. He turns round upon himself, and is specially observant of propriety. The perversity and unreasonableness of the other, however, are still the same. The superior man will again turn round on himself– "I must have been failing to do my utmost."

6. 'He turns round upon himself, and proceeds to do his utmost, but still the perversity and unreasonableness of the other are repeated. On this the superior man says, "This is a man utterly lost indeed! Since he conducts himself so, what is there to choose between him and a brute? Why should I go to contend with a brute?"

7. 'Thus it is that the superior man has a life-long anxiety and not one morning's calamity. As to what is matter of anxiety to him, that indeed he has.– He says, "Shun was a man, and I also am a man. But Shun became an example to all the kingdom, and his conduct was worthy to be handed down to after ages, while I am nothing better than a villager." This indeed is the proper matter of anxiety to him. And in what way is he anxious about it? Just that he may be like Shun:– then only will he stop. As to what the superior man would feel to be a calamity, there is no such thing. He does nothing which is not according to propriety. If there should befall him one morning's calamity, the superior man does not account it a calamity.'

•

1. Yü and Chî, in an age when the world was being brought back to order, thrice passed their doors without entering them. Confucius praised them.

2. The disciple Yen, in an age of disorder, dwelt in a mean narrow lane, having his single bamboo-cup of rice, and his single gourd-dish of water; other men could not have endured the distress, but he did not allow his joy to be affected by it. Confucius praised him.

3. Mencius said, 'Yü, Chî, and Yen Hûi agreed in the principle of their conduct.

4. 'Yü thought that if any one in the kingdom were drowned, it was as if he drowned him. Chî thought that if any one in the kingdom suffered hunger, it was as if he famished him. It was on this account that they were so earnest.

5. If Yü and Chî, and Yen-tsze, had exchanged places, each would have done what the other did.

6. 'Here now in the same apartment with you are people fighting:– you ought to part them. Though you part them with your cap simply tied over your unbound hair, your conduct will be allowable.

7. 'If the fighting be only in the village or neighbourhood, if you go to put an end to it with your cap tied over your hair unbound, you will be in error. Although you should shut your door in such a case, your conduct would be allowable.'

•

1. The disciple Kung-tû said, 'Throughout the whole kingdom everybody

pronounces K'wang Chang unfilial. But you, Master, keep company with him, and moreover treat him with politeness. I venture to ask why you do so.'

2. Mencius replied, 'There are five things which are pronounced in the common usage of the age to be unfilial. The first is laziness in the use of one's four limbs, without attending to the nourishment of his parents. The second is gambling and chess-playing, and being fond of wine, without attending to the nourishment of his parents. The third is being fond of goods and money, and selfishly attached to his wife and children, without attending to the nourishment of his parents. The fourth is following the desires of one's ears and eyes, so as to bring his parents to disgrace. The fifth is being fond of bravery, fighting and quarrelling so as to endanger his parents. Is Chang guilty of any one of these things?

3. 'Now between Chang and his father there arose disagreement, he, the son, reproving his father, to urge him to what was good.

4. 'To urge one another to what is good by reproofs is the way of friends. But such urging between father and son is the greatest injury to the kindness, which should prevail between them.

5. 'Moreover, did not Chang wish to have in his family the relationships of husband and wife, child and mother? But because he had offended his father, and was not permitted to approach him, he sent away his wife, and drove forth his son, and all his life receives no cherishing attention from them. He settled it in his mind that if he did not act in this way, his would be one of the greatest of crimes.– Such and nothing more is the case of Chang.'

•

1. When the philosopher Tsang dwelt in Wû-ch'ang, there came a band from Yüeh to plunder it. Someone said to him, 'The plunderers are coming:– why not leave this?' Tsang on this left the city, saying to the man in charge of the house, 'Do not lodge any persons in my house, lest they break and injure the plants and trees.' When the plunderers withdrew, he sent word to him, saying, 'Repair the walls of my house. I am about to return.' When the plunderers retired, the philosopher Tsang returned accordingly. His disciples said, 'Since our master was treated with so much sincerity and respect, for him to be the first to go away on the arrival of the plunderers, so as to be observed by the people, and then to return on their retiring, appears to us to be improper.' Ch'an-yû Hsing said, 'You do not understand this matter. Formerly, when Ch'an-yû was exposed to the outbreak of the grass-carriers, there were seventy disciples in our master's following, and none of them took part in the matter.'

2. When Tsze-sze was living in Wei, there came a band from Ch'î to plunder. Some one said to him, 'The plunderers are coming;– why not leave this?' Tsze-sze said, 'If I go away, whom will the prince have to guard the State with?'

3. Mencius said, 'The philosophers Tsang and Tsze-sze agreed in the principle of their conduct. Tsang was a teacher;– in the place of a father or elder brother. Tsze-sze was a minister;– in a meaner place. If the philosophers Tsang and Tsze-sze had exchanged places the one would have done what the other did.'

•

1. A man of Ch'î had a wife and a concubine, and lived together with them in his house. When their husband went out, he would get himself well filled with wine and flesh, and then return, and, on his wife's asking him with whom he ate and drank, they were sure to be all wealthy and honourable people. The wife informed the concubine, saying, 'When our good man goes out, he is sure to come back having partaken plentifully of wine and flesh. I asked with whom he ate and drank, and they are all, it seems, wealthy and honourable people. And yet no people of distinction ever come here. I will spy out where our good man goes.'

Accordingly, she got up early in the morning, and privately followed wherever her husband went. Throughout the whole city, there was no one who stood or talked with him. At last, he came to those who were sacrificing among the tombs beyond the outer wall on the east, and begged what they had over. Not being satisfied, he looked about, and went to another party;– and this was the way in which he got himself satiated. His wife returned, and informed the concubine, saying, 'It was to our husband that we looked up in hopeful contemplation, with whom our lot is cast for life;– and now these are his ways!' On this, along with the concubine she reviled their husband, and they wept together in the middle hall. In the meantime the husband, knowing nothing of all this, came in with a jaunty air, carrying himself proudly to his wife and concubine.

2. In the view of a superior man, as to the ways by which men seek for riches, honours, gain, and advancement, there are few of their wives and concubines who would not be ashamed and weep together on account of them.

CHAPTER 17

1. Wan Chang asked Mencius, saying, 'When Shun went into the fields, he cried out and wept towards the pitying heavens. Why did he cry out and weep?' Mencius replied, 'He was dissatisfied, and full of earnest desire.'

2. Wan Chang said, 'When his parents love him, a son rejoices and forgets them not. When his parents hate him, though they punish him, he does not murmur. Was Shun then murmuring against his parents?' Mencius answered, 'Ch'ang Hsî asked Kung-ming Kâo, saying, "As to Shun's going into the fields, I have received your instructions, but I do not know about his weeping and crying out to the pitying heavens and to his parents." Kung-ming Kâo answered him, "You do not understand that matter." Now, Kung-ming Kâo supposed that the heart of the filial son could not be so free of sorrow. Shun would say, "I exert my strength to cultivate the fields, but I am thereby only discharging my office as a son. What can there be in me that my parents do not love me?"

3. 'The Tî caused his own children, nine sons and two daughters, the various officers, oxen and sheep, storehouses and granaries, all to be prepared, to serve Shun amid the channelled fields. Of the scholars of the kingdom there were multitudes who flocked to him. The sovereign designed that Shun should superintend the kingdom along with him, and then to transfer it to him entirely. But because his parents were not in accord with him, he felt like a poor man who has nowhere to turn to.

4. 'To be delighted in by all the scholars of the kingdom, is what men desire, but it was not sufficient to remove the sorrow of Shun. The possession of beauty is what men desire, and Shun had for his wives the two daughters of the Tî, but this was not sufficient to remove his sorrow. Riches are what men desire, and the kingdom was the rich property of Shun, but this was not sufficient to remove his sorrow. Honours are what men desire, and Shun had the dignity of being sovereign, but this was not sufficient to remove his sorrow. The reason why the being the object of men's delight, with the possession of beauty, riches, and honours were not sufficient to remove his sorrow, was that it could be removed only by his getting his parents to be in accord with him.

5. 'The desire of the child is towards his father and mother. When he becomes conscious of the attractions of beauty, his desire is towards young and beautiful women. When he comes to have a wife and children, his desire is towards them. When he obtains office, his desire is towards his sovereign:– if he cannot get the regard of his sovereign, he burns within. But the man of great filial piety, to the

end of his life, has his desire towards his parents. In the great Shun I see the case of one whose desire at fifty years was towards them.'

●

1. Wan Chang asked Mencius, saying, 'It is said in the Book of Poetry,

In marrying a wife, how ought a man to proceed?
He must inform his parents.

If the rule be indeed as here expressed, no man ought to have illustrated it so well as Shun. How was it that Shun's marriage took place without his informing his parents?' Mencius replied, 'If he had informed them, he would not have been able to marry. That male and female should dwell together, is the greatest of human relations. If Shun had informed his parents, he must have made void this greatest of human relations, thereby incurring their resentment. On this account, he did not inform them!

2. Wan Chang said, 'As to Shun's marrying without informing his parents, I have heard your instructions; but how was it that the Tî Yâo gave him his daughters as wives without informing Shun's parents?' Mencius said, 'The Tî also knew that if he informed them, he could not marry his daughters to him.'

3. Wan Chang said, 'His parents set Shun to repair a granary, to which, the ladder having been removed, Kû-sâu set fire. They also made him dig a well. He got out, but they, not knowing that, proceeded to cover him up. Hsiang said, "Of the scheme to cover up the city-forming prince, the merit is all mine. Let my parents have his oxen and sheep. Let them have his storehouses and granaries. His shield and spear shall be mine. His lute shall be mine. His bow shall be mine. His two wives I shall make attend for me to my bed." Hsiang then went away into Shun's palace, and there was Shun on his couch playing on his lute. Hsiang said, "I am come simply because I was thinking anxiously about you." At the same time, he blushed deeply. Shun said to him, "There are all my officers:– do you undertake the government of them for me." I do not know whether Shun was ignorant of Hsiang's wishing to kill him.' Mencius answered, 'How could he be ignorant of that? But when Hsiang was sorrowful, he was also sorrowful; when Hsiang was joyful, he was also joyful.'

4. Chang said, 'In that case, then, did not Shun rejoice hypocritically?' Mencius replied, 'No. Formerly, some one sent a present of a live fish to Tsze-ch'an of Chang. Tsze-ch'an ordered his pond-keeper to keep it in the pond, but that officer cooked it, and reported the execution of his commission, saying, "When I first let it go, it appeared embarrassed. In a little while, it seemed to be somewhat at ease, then it swam away joyfully." Tsze-ch'an observed, "It had got into its element! It had got into its element!" The pond-keeper then went out and

said, "Who calls Tsze-ch'an a wise man? After I had cooked and eaten the fish, he says, "It had got into its element! It had got into its element!"' Thus a superior man may be imposed on by what seems to be as it ought to be, but he cannot be entrapped by what is contrary to right principle. Hsiang came in the way in which the love of his elder brother would have made him come; therefore Shun sincerely believed him, and rejoiced. What hypocrisy was there?'

•

1. Wan Chang said, 'Hsiang made it his daily business to slay Shun. When Shun was made sovereign, how was it that he only banished him?' Mencius said, 'He raised him to be a prince. Some supposed that it was banishing him?'

2. Wan Chang said, 'Shun banished the superintendent of works to Yû-châu; he sent away Hwan-tâu to the mountain Ch'ung; he slew the prince of San-miâo in San-wei; and he imprisoned Kwân on the mountain Yü. When the crimes of those four were thus punished, the whole kingdom acquiesced:– it was a cutting off of men who were destitute of benevolence. But Hsiang was of all men the most destitute of benevolence, and Shun raised him to be the prince of Yû-pî;– of what crimes had the people of Yû-pî been guilty? Does a benevolent man really act thus? In the case of other men, he cut them off; in the case of his brother, he raised him to be a prince.' Mencius replied, 'A benevolent man does not lay up anger, nor cherish resentment against his brother, but only regards him with affection and love. Regarding him with affection, he wishes him to be honourable: regarding him with love, he wishes him to be rich. The appointment of Hsiang to be the prince of Yû-pî was to enrich and ennoble him. If while Shun himself was sovereign, his brother had been a common man, could he have been said to regard him with affection and love?'

3. Wan Chang said, 'I venture to ask what you mean by saying that some supposed that it was a banishing of Hsiang?' Mencius replied, 'Hsiang could do nothing in his State. The Son of Heaven appointed an officer to administer its government, and to pay over its revenues to him. This treatment of him led to its being said that he was banished. How indeed could he be allowed the means of oppressing the people? Nevertheless, Shun wished to be continually seeing him, and by this arrangement, he came incessantly to court, as is signified in that expression– "He did not wait for the rendering of tribute, or affairs of government, to receive the prince of Yû-pî.

•

1. Hsien-ch'iû Mang asked Mencius, saying, 'There is the saying, "A scholar of complete virtue may not be employed as a minister by his sovereign, nor treated as a son by his father. Shun stood with his face to the south, and Yâo,

at the head of all the princes, appeared before him at court with his face to the north. Kû-sâu also did the same. When Shun saw Kû-sâu, his countenance became discomposed. Confucius said, At this time, in what a perilous condition was the kingdom! Its state was indeed unsettled."– I do not know whether what is here said really took place.' Mencius replied, 'No. These are not the words of a superior man. They are the sayings of an uncultivated person of the east of Ch'î. When Yâo was old, Shun was associated with him in the government. It is said in the Canon of Yâo, "After twenty and eight years, the Highly Meritorious one deceased. The people acted as if they were mourning for a father or mother for three years, and up to the borders of the four seas every sound of music was hushed." Confucius said, "There are not two suns in the sky, nor two sovereigns over the people." Shun having been sovereign, and, moreover, leading on all the princes to observe the three years' mourning for Yâo, there would have been in this case two sovereigns.'

2. Hsien-ch'iû Mang said, 'On the point of Shun's not treating Yâo as a minister, I have received your instructions. But it is said in the Book of Poetry,

> Under the whole heaven,
> Every spot is the sovereign's ground;
> To the borders of the land,
> Every individual is the sovereign's minister;

– and Shun had become sovereign. I venture to ask how it was that Kû-sâu was not one of his ministers.' Mencius answered, 'That ode is not to be understood in that way:– it speaks of being laboriously engaged in the sovereign's business, so as not to be able to nourish one's parents, as if the author said, "This is all the sovereign's business, and how is it that I alone am supposed to have ability, and am made to toil in it?" Therefore, those who explain the odes, may not insist on one term so as to do violence to a sentence, nor on a sentence so as to do violence to the general scope. They must try with their thoughts to meet that scope, and then we shall apprehend it. If we simply take single sentences, there is that in the ode called "The Milky Way,"–

> Of the black-haired people of the remnant of Châu,
> There is not half a one left.

If it had been really as thus expressed, then not an individual of the people of Châu was left.

3. 'Of all which a filial son can attain to, there is nothing greater than his honouring his parents. And of what can be attained to in the honouring one's parents, there is nothing greater than the nourishing them with the whole kingdom. Kû-sâu was the father of the sovereign;– this was the height of honour.

Shun nourished him with the whole kingdom;– this was the height of nourishing. In this was verified the sentiment in the Book of Poetry,

> *Ever cherishing filial thoughts,*
> *Those filial thoughts became an example to after ages.*

4. 'It is said in the Book of History, "Reverently performing his duties, he waited on Kû-sâu, and was full of veneration and awe. Kû-sâu also believed him and conformed to virtue."– This is the true case of the scholar of complete virtue not being treated as a son by his father.'

CHAPTER 18

1. Wan Chang said, 'Was it the case that Yâo gave the throne to Shun?' Mencius said, 'No. The sovereign cannot give the throne to another.'

2. 'Yes;– but Shun had the throne. Who gave it to him?' 'Heaven gave it to him,' was the answer.

3. '" Heaven gave it to him:"– did Heaven confer its appointment on him with specific injunctions?'

4. Mencius replied, 'No. Heaven does not speak. It simply showed its will by his personal conduct and his conduct of affairs.'

5. '"It showed its will by his personal conduct and his conduct of affairs:"– how was this?' Mencius's answer was, 'The sovereign can present a man to Heaven, but he cannot make Heaven give that man the throne. A prince can present a man to the sovereign, but he cannot cause the sovereign to make that man a prince. A great officer can present a man to his prince, but he cannot cause the prince to make that man a great officer. Yâo presented Shun to Heaven, and Heaven accepted him. He presented him to the people, and the people accepted him. Therefore I say, "Heaven does not speak. It simply indicated its will by his personal conduct and his conduct of affairs."'

6. Chang said, 'I presume to ask how it was that Yâo presented Shun to Heaven, and Heaven accepted him; and that he exhibited him to the people, and the people accepted him.' Mencius replied, 'He caused him to preside over the sacrifices, and all the spirits were well pleased with them;– thus Heaven accepted him. He caused him to preside over the conduct of affairs, and affairs were well administered, so that the people reposed under him;– thus the people accepted him. Heaven gave the throne to him. The people gave it to him. Therefore I said, "The sovereign cannot give the throne to another."

7. 'Shun assisted Yâo in the government for twenty and eight years;– this was more than man could have done, and was from Heaven. After the death of Yâo, when the three years' mourning was completed, Shun withdrew from the son of Yâo to the south of South river. The princes of the kingdom, however, repairing to court, went not to the son of Yâo, but they went to Shun. Litigants went not to the son of Yâo, but they went to Shun. Singers sang not the son of Yâo, but they sang Shun. Therefore I said, "Heaven gave him the throne." It was after these things that he went to the Middle Kingdom, and occupied the seat of the Son of Heaven. If he had, before these things, taken up his residence in the

palace of Yâo, and had applied pressure to the son of Yâo, it would have been an act of usurpation, and not the gift of Heaven.

8. 'This sentiment is expressed in the words of The Great Declaration,– "Heaven sees according as my people see; Heaven hears according as my people hear."'

•

1. Wan Chang asked Mencius, saying, 'People say, "When the disposal of the kingdom came to Yü, his virtue was inferior to that of Yâo and Shun, and he transmitted it not to the worthiest but to his son." Was it so?' Mencius replied, 'No; it was not so. When Heaven gave the kingdom to the worthiest, it was given to the worthiest. When Heaven gave it to the son of the preceding sovereign, it was given to him. Shun presented Yü to Heaven. Seventeen years elapsed, and Shun died. When the three years' mourning was expired, Yü withdrew from the son of Shun to Yang-ch'ang. The people of the kingdom followed him just as after the death of Yâo, instead of following his son, they had followed Shun. Yü presented Yî to Heaven. Seven years elapsed, and Yü died. When the three years' mourning was expired, Yî withdrew from the son of Yü to the north of mount Ch'î. The princes, repairing to court, went not to Yî, but they went to Ch'î. Litigants did not go to Yî, but they went to Ch'î, saying, "He is the son of our sovereign;" the singers did not sing Yî, but they sang Ch'î, saying, "He is the son of our sovereign."

2. 'That Tan-chû was not equal to his father, and Shun's son not equal to his; that Shun assisted Yâo, and Yü assisted Shun, for many years, conferring benefits on the people for a long time; that thus the length of time during which Shun, Yü, and Yî assisted in the government was so different; and that the sons of the emperors were - the one a man of talents and virtue, and the other two inferior to their fathers:– all this was from Heaven, and what could not be brought about by man. That which is done without man's doing is from Heaven. That which happens without man's causing is from the ordinance of Heaven.

3. 'In the case of a private individual obtaining the throne, there must be in him virtue equal to that of Shun or Yü; and moreover there must be the presenting of him to Heaven by the preceding sovereign. It was on this account that Confucius did not obtain the throne.

4. 'When the kingdom is possessed by natural succession, the sovereign who is displaced by Heaven must be like Chieh or Châu. It was on this account that Yî, Î Yin, and Châu-kung did not obtain the throne.

5. 'Î Yin assisted T'ang so that he became sovereign over the kingdom. After the demise of T'ang, T'âi-ting having died before he could be appointed sovereign, Wâ'i-ping reigned two years, and Chung-zin four. T'âi-chiâ was then

turning upside down the statutes of T'ang, when Î Yin placed him in T'ung for three years. There T'âi-chiâ repented of his errors, was contrite, and reformed himself. In T'ung be came to dwell in benevolence and walk in righteousness, during those threee years, listening to the lessons given to him by Î Yin. Then Î Yin again returned with him to Po.

6. 'Châu-kung not getting the throne was like the case of Yî and the throne of Hsiâ, or like that of Î Yin and the throne of Yin.

7. 'Confucius said, "T'ang and Yü resigned the throne to their worthy ministers. The sovereign of Hsiâ and those of Yin and Châu transmitted it to their sons. The principle of righteousness was the same in all the cases."'

•

1. Wan Chang asked Mencius, saying, 'People say that Î Yin sought an introduction to T'ang by his knowledge of cookery. Was it so?'

2. Mencius replied, 'No, it was not so. Î Yin was a farmer in the lands of the prince of Hsin, delighting in the principles of Yâo and Shun. In any matter contrary to the righteousness which they prescribed, or contrary to their principles, though he had been offered the throne, he would not have regarded it; though there had been yoked for him a thousand teams of horses, he would not have looked at them. In any matter contrary to the righteousness which they prescribed, or contrary to their principles, he would neither have given nor taken a single straw.

3. 'T'ang sent persons with presents of silk to entreat him to enter his service. With an air of indifference and self-satisfaction he said, "What can I do with those silks with which T'ang invites me? Is it not best for me to abide in the channelled fields, and so delight myself with the principles of Yâo and Shun?"

4. 'T'ang thrice sent messengers to invite him. After this, with the change of resolution displayed in his countenance, he spoke in a different style,– "Instead of abiding in the channelled fields and thereby delighting myself with the principles of Yâo and Shun, had I not better make this prince a prince like Yâo or Shun, and this people like the people of Yâo or Shun ? Had I not better in my own person see these things for myself?

5. '"Heaven's plan in the production of mankind is this:– that they who are first informed should instruct those who are later in being informed, and they who first apprehend principles should instruct those who are slower to do so. I am one of Heaven's people who have first apprehended;– I will take these principles and instruct this people in them. If I do not instruct them, who will do so?"

6. 'He thought that among all the people of the kingdom, even the private men and women, if there were any who did not enjoy such benefits as Yâo and Shun conferred, it was as if he himself pushed them into a ditch. He took upon himself the heavy charge of the kingdom in this way, and therefore he went to T'ang, and pressed upon him the subject of attacking Hsiâ and saving the people.

7. 'I have not heard of one who bent himself, and at the same time made others straight;– how much less could one disgrace himself, and thereby rectify the whole kingdom? The actions of the sages have been different. Some have kept remote from court, and some have drawn near to it; some have left their offices, and some have not done so:– that to which those different courses all agree is simply the keeping of their persons pure.

8. 'I have heard that Î Yin sought an introduction to T'ang by the doctrines of Yâo and Shun. I have not heard that he did so by his knowledge of cookery.

9. 'In the "Instructions of Î," it is said, "Heaven destroying Chieh commenced attacking him in the palace of Mû. I commenced in Po."'

•

1. Wan Chang asked Mencius, saying, 'Some say that Confucius, when he was in Wei, lived with the ulcer-doctor, and when he was in Ch'î, with the attendant, Ch'î Hwan;– was it so?' Mencius replied, 'No; it was not so. Those are the inventions of men fond of strange things.

2. 'When he was in Wei, he lived with Yen Ch'âu-yû. The wives of the officer Mî and Tsze-lû were sisters, and Mî told Tsze-lû, "If Confucius will lodge with me, he may attain to the dignity of a high noble of Wei." Tsze-lû informed Confucius of this, and he said, "That is as ordered by Heaven." Confucius went into office according to propriety, and retired from it according to righteousness. In regard to his obtaining office or not obtaining it, he said, "That is as ordered." But if he had lodged with the attendant Chî Hwan, that would neither have been according to righteousness, nor any ordering of Heaven.

3. 'When Confucius, being dissatisfied in Lû and Wei, had left those States, he met with the attempt of Hwan, the Master of the Horse, of Sung, to intercept and kill him. He assumed, however, the dress of a common man, and passed by Sung. At that time, though he was in circumstances of distress, he lodged with the city-master Ch'ang, who was then a minister of Châu, the marquis of Ch'an.

4. 'I have heard that the characters of ministers about court may be discerned from those whom they entertain, and those of stranger officers, from those with whom they lodge. If Confucius had lodged with the ulcer-doctor, and with the attendant Chî Hwan, how could he have been Confucius?'

1. Wan Chang asked Mencius, 'Some say that Pâi-lî Hsî sold himself to a cattle-keeper of Ch'in for the skins of five rams, and fed his oxen, in order to find an introduction to the duke Mû of Ch'in;– was this the case?' Mencius said, 'No; it was not so. This story was inverted by men fond of strange things.

2. 'Pâi-lî Hsî was a man of Yü. The people of Tsin, by the inducement of a round piece of jade from Ch'ûi-chî, and four horses of the Ch'ü breed, borrowed a passage through Yü to attack Kwo. On that occasion, Kung Chih-ch'î remonstrated against granting their request, and Pâi-lî Hsî did not remonstrate.

3. 'When he knew that the duke of Yü was not to be remonstrated with, and, leaving that State, went to Ch'in, he had reached the age of seventy. If by that time he did not know that it would be a mean thing to seek an introduction to the duke Mû of Ch'in by feeding oxen, could he be called wise? But not remonstrating where it was of no use to remonstrate, could he be said not to be wise? Knowing that the duke of Yü would be ruined, and leaving him before that event, he cannot be said not to have been wise. Being then advanced in Ch'in, he knew that the duke Mû was one with whom he would enjoy a field for action, and became minister to him;– could he, acting thus, be said not to be wise? Having become chief minister of Ch'in, he made his prince distinguished throughout the kingdom, and worthy of being handed down to future ages;– could he have done this, if he had not been a man of talents and virtue? As to selling himself in order to accomplish all the aims of his prince, even a villager who had a regard for himself would not do such a thing; and shall we say that a man of talents and virtue did it?'

CHAPTER 19

1. Mencius said, 'Po-î would not allow his eyes to look on a bad sight, nor his ears to listen to a bad sound. He would not serve a prince whom he did not approve, nor command a people whom he did not esteem. In a time of good government he took office, and on the occurrence of confusion he retired. He could not bear to dwell either in a court from which a lawless government emanated, or among lawless people. He considered his being in the same place with a villager, as if he were to sit amid mud and coals with his court robes and court cap. In the time of Châu he dwelt on the shores of the North sea, waiting the purification of the kingdom. Therefore when men now hear the character of Po-î, the corrupt become pure, and the weak acquire determination.

2. 'Î Yin said, "Whom may I not serve? My serving him makes him my sovereign. What people may I not command? My commanding them makes them my people." In a time of good government he took office, and when confusion prevailed, he also took office. He said, "Heaven's plan in the production of mankind is this:– that they who are first informed should instruct those who are later in being informed, and they who first apprehend principles should instruct those who are slower in doing so. I am the one of Heaven's people who has first apprehended;– I will take these principles and instruct the people in them." He thought that among all the people of the kingdom, even the common men and women, if there were any who did not share in the enjoyment of such benefits as Yâo and Shun conferred, it was as if he himself pushed them into a ditch;– for he took upon himself the heavy charge of the kingdom.

3. 'Hûi of Liû-hsiâ was not ashamed to serve an impure prince, nor did he think it low to be an inferior officer. When advanced to employment, he did not conceal his virtue, but made it a point to carry out his principles. When dismissed and left without office, he did not murmur. When straitened by poverty, he did not grieve. When thrown into the company of village people, he was quite at ease and could not bear to leave them. He had a saying, "You are you, and I am I. Although you stand by my side with breast and arms bare, or with your body naked, how can you defile me?" Therefore when men now hear the character of Hûi of Liü-hsiâ, the mean become generous, and the niggardly become liberal.

4. 'When Confucius was leaving Ch'î, he strained off with his hand the water in which his rice was being rinsed, took the rice, and went away. When he left Lû, he said, "I will set out by-and-by:"– it was right he should leave the country of his parents in this way. When it was proper to go away quickly, he did so;

when it was proper to delay, he did so; when it was proper to keep in retirement, he did so; when it was proper to go into office, he did so:– this was Confucius.'

5. Mencius said,'Po-î among the sages was the pure one; Î Yin was the one most inclined to take office; Hûi of Liû-hsiâ was the accommodating one; and Confucius was the timeous one.

6. 'In Confucius we have what is called a complete concert. A complete concert is when the large bell proclaims the commencement of the music, and the ringing stone proclaims its close. The metal sound commences the blended harmony of all the instruments, and the winding up with the stone terminates that blended harmony. The commencing that harmony is the work of wisdom. The terminating it is the work of sageness.

7. 'As a comparison for wisdom, we may liken it to skill, and as a comparison for sageness, we may liken it to strength;– as in the case of shooting at a mark a hundred paces distant. That you reach it is owing to your strength, but that you hit the mark is not owing to your strength.'

•

1. Pêi-kung Î asked Mencius, saying, 'What was the arrangement of dignities and emoluments determined by the House of Châu?'

2. Mencius replied, 'The particulars of that arrangement cannot be learned, for the princes, disliking them as injurious to themselves, have all made away with the records of them. Still I have learned the general outline of them.

3. 'The SON OF HEAVEN constituted one dignity; the KUNG one; the HÂU one; the PÂI one; and the TSZE and the NAN each one of equal rank:– altogether making five degrees of rank. The RULER again constituted one dignity; the CHIEF MINISTER one; the GREAT OFFICERS one; the SCHOLARS OF THE FIRST CLASS one; THOSE OF THE MIDDLE CLASS one; and THOSE OF THE LOWEST CLASS one:– altogether making six degrees of dignity.

4. 'To the Son of Heaven there was allotted a territory of a thousand lî square. A Kung and a Hâu had each a hundred lî square. A Pâi had seventy lî, and a Tsze and a Nan had each fifty lî. The assignments altogether were of four amounts. Where the territory did not amount to fifty lî, the chief could not have access himself to the Son of Heaven. His land was attached to some Hâu-ship, and was called a FÛ-YUNG.

5. 'The Chief ministers of the Son of Heaven received an amount of territory equal to that of a Hâu; a Great officer received as much as a Pâi; and a scholar of the first class as much as a Tsze or a Nan.

6. 'In a great State, where the territory was a hundred lî square, the ruler had

ten times as much income as his Chief ministers; a Chief minister four times as much as a Great officer; a Great officer twice as much as a scholar of the first class; a scholar of the first class twice as much as one of the middle; a scholar of the middle class twice as much as one of the lowest; the scholars of the lowest class, and such of the common people as were employed about the government offices, had for their emolument as much as was equal to what they would have made by tilling the fields.

7. 'In a State of the next order, where the territory was seventy lî square, the ruler had ten times as much revenue as his Chief minister; a Chief minister three times as much as a Great officer; a Great officer twice as much as a scholar of the first class; a scholar of the first class twice as much as one of the middle; a scholar of the middle class twice as much as one of the lowest; the scholars of the lowest class, and such of the common people as were employed about the government offices, had for their emolument as much as was equal to what they would have made by tilling the fields.

8. 'In a small State, where the territory was fifty lî square, the ruler had ten times as much revenue as his Chief minister; a Chief minister had twice as much as a Great officer; a Great officer twice as much as a scholar of the highest class; a scholar of the highest class twice as much as one of the middle; a scholar of the middle class twice as much as one of the lowest; scholars of the lowest class, and such of the common people as were employed about the government offices, had the same emolument;– as much, namely, as was equal to what they would have made by tilling the fields.

9. 'As to those who tilled the fields, each husbandman received a hundred mâu. When those mâu were manured, the best husbandmen of the highest class supported nine individuals, and those ranking next to them supported eight. The best husbandmen of the second class supported seven individuals, and those ranking next to them supported six; while husbandmen of the lowest class only supported five. The salaries of the common people who were employed about the government offices were regulated according to these differences.'

•

1. Wan Chang asked Mencius, saying, 'I venture to ask the principles of friendship.' Mencius replied, 'Friendship should be maintained without any presumption on the ground of one's superior age, or station, or the circumstances of his relatives. Friendship with a man is friendship with his virtue, and does not admit of assumptions of superiority.

2. 'There was Mang Hsien, chief of a family of a hundred chariots. He had five friends, namely, Yo-chang Chiû, Mû Chung, and three others whose names I

have forgotten. With those five men Hsien maintained a friendship, because they thought nothing about his family. If they had thought about his family, he would not have maintained his friendship with them.

3. 'Not only has the chief of a family of a hundred chariots acted thus. The same thing was exemplified by the sovereign of a small State. The duke Hûi of Pî said, "I treat Tsze-sze as my Teacher, and Yen Pan as my Friend. As to Wang Shun and Ch'ang Hsî, they serve me."

4. 'Not only has the sovereign of a small State acted thus. The same thing has been exemplified by the sovereign of a large State. There was the duke P'ing of Tsin with Hâi T'ang:– when T'ang told him to come into his house, he came; when he told him to be seated, he sat; when he told him to eat, he ate. There might only be coarse rice and soup of vegetables, but he always ate his fill, not daring to do otherwise. Here, however, he stopped, and went no farther. He did not call him to share any of Heaven's places, or to govern any of Heaven's offices, or to partake of any of Heaven's emoluments. His conduct was but a scholar's honouring virtue and talents, not the honouring them proper to a king or a duke.

5. 'Shun went up to court and saw the sovereign, who lodged him as his son-in-law in the second palace. The sovereign also enjoyed there Shun's hospitality. Alternately he was host and guest. Here was the sovereign maintaining friendship with a private man.

6. Respect shown by inferiors to superiors is called giving to the noble the observance due to rank. Respect shown by superiors to inferiors is called giving honour to talents and virtue. The rightness in each case is the same.'

•

1. Wan Chang asked Mencius, saying, 'I venture to ask what feeling of the mind is expressed in the presents of friendship?' Mencius replied, 'The feeling of respect.'

2. 'How is it,' pursued Chang, 'that the declining a present is accounted disrespectful?' The answer was, 'When one of honourable rank presents a gift, to say in the mind, "Was the way in which he got this righteous or not? I must know this before I can receive it;"– this is deemed disrespectful, and therefore presents are not declined.'

3. Wan Chang asked again, 'When one does not take on him in so many express words to refuse the gift, but having declined it in his heart, saying, "It was taken by him unrighteously from the people," and then assigns some other reason for not receiving it;– is not this a proper course?' Mencius said, 'When the donor offers it on a ground of reason, and his manner of doing so is according to propriety;– in such a case Confucius would have received it.'

4. Wan Chang said, 'Here now is one who stops and robs people outside the gates of the city. He offers his gift on a ground of reason, and does so in a manner according to propriety;– would the reception of it so acquired by robbery be proper?' Mencius replied, 'It would not be proper. In "The Announcement to Kang" it is said, "When men kill others, and roll over their bodies to take their property, being reckless and fearless of death, among all the people there are none but detest them:"– thus, such characters are to be put to death, without waiting to give them warning. Yin received this rule from Hsiâ and Châu received it from Yin. It cannot be questioned, and to the present day is clearly acknowledged. How can the gift of a robber be received?'

5. Chang said, 'The princes of the present day take from their people just as a robber despoils his victim. Yet if they put a good face of propriety on their gifts, then the superior man receives them. I venture to ask how you explain this.' Mencius answered, 'Do you think that, if there should arise a truly royal sovereign, he would collect the princes of the present day, and put them all to death? Or would he admonish them, and then, on their not changing their ways, put them to death? Indeed, to call every one who takes what does not properly belong to him a robber, is pushing a point of resemblance to the utmost, and insisting on the most refined idea of righteousness. When Confucius was in office in Lû, the people struggled together for the game taken in hunting, and he also did the same. If that struggling for the captured game was proper, how much more may the gifts of the princes be received!'

6. Chang urged, 'Then are we to suppose that when Confucius held office, it was not with the view to carry his doctrines into practice?' 'It was with that view,' Mencius replied, and Chang rejoined, 'If the practice of his doctrines was his business, what had he to do with that struggling for the captured game?' Mencius said, 'Confucius first rectified his vessels of sacrifice according to the registers, and did not fill them so rectified with food gathered from every quarter.' 'But why did he not go away?' He wished to make a trial of carrying his doctrines into practice. When that trial was sufficient to show that they could be practised and they were still not practised, then he went away, and thus it was that he never completed in any State a residence of three years.

7. 'Confucius took office when he saw that the practice of his doctrines was likely; he took office when his reception was proper; he took office when he was supported by the State. In the case of his relation to Chî Hwan, he took office, seeing that the practice of his doctrines was likely. With the duke Ling of Wei he took office, because his reception was proper. With the duke Hsiâo of Wei he took office, because he was maintained by the State.'

CHAPTER 20

1. Mencius said, 'Office is not sought on account of poverty, yet there are times when one seeks office on that account. Marriage is not entered into for the sake of being attended to by the wife, yet there are times when one marries on that account.

2. 'He who takes office on account of his poverty must decline an honourable situation and occupy a low one; he must decline riches and prefer to be poor.

3. 'What office will be in harmony with this declining an honourable situation and occupying a low one, this declining riches and preferring to be poor? Such an one as that of guarding the gates, or beating the watchman's stick.

4. 'Confucius was once keeper of stores, and he then said, "My calculations must be all right. That is all I have to care about." He was once in charge of the public fields, and he then said, "The oxen and sheep must be fat and strong, and superior. That is all I have to care about."

5. 'When one is in a low situation, to speak of high matters is a crime. When a scholar stands in a prince's court, and his principles are not carried into practice, it is a shame to him.'

•

1. Wan Chang said, 'What is the reason that a scholar does not accept a stated support from a prince?' Mencius replied, 'He does not presume to do so. When a prince loses his State, and then accepts a stated support from another prince, this is in accordance with propriety. But for a scholar to accept such support from any of the princes is not in accordance with propriety.'

2. Wan Chang said, 'If the prince send him a present of grain, for instance, does he accept it?' 'He accepts it,' answered Mencius. 'On what principle of righteousness does he accept it?' 'Why– the prince ought to assist the people in their necessities.'

3. Chang pursued, 'Why is it that the scholar will thus accept the prince's help, but will not accept his pay?' The answer was, 'He does not presume to do so.' 'I venture to ask why he does not presume to do so.' 'Even the keepers of the gates, with their watchmen's sticks, have their regular offices for which they can take their support from the prince. He who without a regular office should receive the pay of the prince must be deemed disrespectful.'

4. Chang asked, 'If the prince sends a scholar a present, he accepts it;– I do not know whether this present may be constantly repeated.' Mencius answered,

'There was the conduct of the duke Mû to Tsze-sze– He made frequent inquiries after Tsze-sze's health, and sent him frequent presents of cooked meat. Tsze-sze was displeased; and at length, having motioned to the messenger to go outside the great door, he bowed his head to the ground with his face to the north, did obeisance twice, and declined the gift, saying, "From this time forth I shall know that the prince supports me as a dog or a horse." And so from that time a servant was no more sent with the presents. When a prince professes to be pleased with a man of talents and virtue, and can neither promote him to office, nor support him in the proper way, can he be said to be pleased with him?

5. Chang said, 'I venture to ask how the sovereign of a State, when he wishes to support a superior man, must proceed, that he may be said to do so in the proper way?' Mencius answered, 'At first, the present must be offered with the prince's commission, and the scholar, making obeisance twice with his head bowed to the ground, will receive it. But after this the storekeeper will continue to send grain, and the master of the kitchen to send meat, presenting it as if without the prince's express commission. Tsze-sze considered that the meat from the prince's cauldron, giving him the annoyance of constantly doing obeisance, was not the way to support a superior man.

6. 'There was Yâo's conduct to Shun:– He caused his nine sons to serve him, and gave him his two daughters in marriage; he caused the various officers, oxen and sheep, storehouses and granaries, all to be prepared to support Shun amid the channelled fields, and then he raised him to the most exalted situation. From this we have the expression– "The honouring of virtue and talents proper to a king or a duke."'

•

1. Wan Chang said, 'I venture to ask what principle of righteousness is involved in a scholar's not going to see the princes?' Mencius replied, 'A scholar residing in the city is called "a minister of the market-place and well," and one residing in the country is called "a minister of the grass and plants." In both cases he is a common man, and it is the rule of propriety that common men, who have not presented the introductory present and become ministers, should not presume to have interviews with the prince.'

2. Wan Chang said, 'If a common man is called to perform any service, he goes and performs it;– how is it that a scholar, when the prince, wishing to see him, calls him to his presence, refuses to go?' Mencius replied, 'It is right to go and perform the service; it would not be right to go and see the prince.'

3. 'And,' added Mencius, 'on what account is it that the prince wishes to see the scholar?' 'Because of his extensive information, or because of his talents and

virtue,' was the reply. 'If because of his extensive information,' said Mencius, 'such a person is a teacher, and the sovereign would not call him;– how much less may any of the princes do so? If because of his talents and virtue, then I have not heard of any one wishing to see a person with those qualities, and calling him to his presence.

4. 'During the frequent interviews of the duke Mû with Tsze-sze, he one day said to him, "Anciently, princes of a thousand chariots have yet been on terms of friendship with scholars;– what do you think of such an intercourse?" Tsze-sze was displeased, and said, "The ancients have said, 'The scholar should be served:' how should they have merely said that he should be made a friend of?" When Tsze-sze was thus displeased, did he not say within himself,– "With regard to our stations, you are sovereign, and I am subject. How can I presume to be on terms of friendship with my sovereign! With regard to our virtue, you ought to make me your master. How can you be on terms of friendship with me?" Thus, when a ruler of a thousand chariots sought to be on terms of friendship with a scholar, he could not obtain his wish:– how much less could he call him to his presence!

5. 'The duke Ching of Ch'î, once, when he was hunting, called his forester to him by a flag. The forester would not come, and the duke was going to kill him. With reference to this incident, Confucius said, "The determined officer never forgets that his end may be in a ditch or a stream; the brave officer never forgets that he may lose his head." What was it in the forester that Confucius thus approved? He approved his not going to the duke, when summoned by the article which was not appropriate to him.'

6. Chang said, 'May I ask with what a forester should be summoned?' Mencius replied, 'With a skin cap. A common man should be summoned with a plain banner; a scholar who has taken office, with one having dragons embroidered on it; and a Great officer, with one having feathers suspended from the top of the staff.

7. 'When the forester was summoned with the article appropriate to the summoning of a Great officer, he would have died rather than presume to go. If a common man were summoned with the article appropriate to the summoning of a scholar, how could he presume to go? How much more may we expect this refusal to go, when a man of talents and virtue is summoned in a way which is inappropriate to his character!

8. 'When a prince wishes to see a man of talents and virtue, and does not take the proper course to get his wish, it is as if he wished him to enter his palace, and shut the door against him. Now, righteousness is the way, and propriety is the door, but it is only the superior man who can follow this way, and go out and in by this door. It is said in the Book of Poetry,

The way to Châu is level like a whetstone,
And straight as an arrow.
The officers tread it,
And the lower people see it.

9. Wan Chang said, 'When Confucius received the prince's message calling him, he went without waiting for his carriage. Doing so, did Confucius do wrong?' Mencius replied, 'Confucius was in office, and had to observe its appropriate duties. And moreover, he was summoned on the business of his office.'

•

1. Mencius said to Wan Chang, 'The scholar whose virtue is most distinguished in a village shall make friends of all the virtuous scholars in the village. The scholar whose virtue is most distinguished throughout a State shall make friends of all the virtuous scholars of that State. The scholar whose virtue is most distinguished throughout the kingdom shall make friends of all the virtuous scholars of the kingdom.

2. 'When a scholar feels that his friendship with all the virtuous scholars of the kingdom is not sufficient to satisfy him, he proceeds to ascend to consider the men of antiquity. He repeats their poems, and reads their books, and as he does not know what they were as men, to ascertain this, he considers their history. This is to ascend and make friends of the men of antiquity.'

•

1. The king Hsüan of Ch'î asked about the office of high ministers. Mencius said, 'Which high ministers is your Majesty asking about?' 'Are there differences among them?' inquired the king. 'There are' was the reply. 'There are the high ministers who are noble and relatives of the prince, and there are those who are of a different surname.' The king said, 'I beg to ask about the high ministers who are noble and relatives of the prince.' Mencius answered, 'If the prince have great faults, they ought to remonstrate with him, and if he do not listen to them after they have done so again and again, they ought to dethrone him.'

2. The king on this looked moved, and changed countenance.

3. Mencius said, 'Let not your Majesty be offended. You asked me, and I dare not answer but according to truth.'

4. The king's countenance became composed, and he then begged to ask about high ministers who were of a different surname from the prince. Mencius said, 'When the prince has faults, they ought to remonstrate with him; and if he do not listen to them after they have done this again and again, they ought to leave the State.'

CHAPTER 21

1. The philosopher Kâo said, 'Man's nature is like the ch'î-willow , and righteousness is like a cup or a bowl. The fashioning benevolence and righteousness out of man's nature is like the making cups and bowls from the ch'î-willow.'

2. Mencius replied, 'Can you, leaving untouched the nature of the willow, make with it cups and bowls? You must do violence and injury to the willow, before you can make cups and bowls with it. If you must do violence and injury to the willow in order to make cups and bowls with it, on your principles you must in the same way do violence and injury to humanity in order to fashion from it benevolence and righteousness! Your words, alas! would certainly lead all men on to reckon benevolence and righteousness to be calamities.'

●

1. The philosopher Kâo said, 'Man's nature is like water whirling round in a corner. Open a passage for it to the east, and it will flow to the east; open a passage for it to the west, and it will flow to the west. Man's nature is indifferent to good and evil, just as the water is indifferent to the east and west.'

2. Mencius replied, 'Water indeed will flow indifferently to the east or west, but will it flow indifferently up or down? The tendency of man's nature to good is like the tendency of water to flow downwards. There are none but have this tendency to good, just as all water flows downwards.

3. 'Now by striking water and causing it to leap up, you may make it go over your forehead, and, by damming and leading it you may force it up a hill;– but are such movements according to the nature of water? It is the force applied which causes them. When men are made to do what is not good, their nature is dealt with in this way.'

●

1. The philosopher Kâo said, 'Life is what is to be understood by nature!'

2. Mencius asked him, 'Do you say that by nature you mean life, just as you say that white is white?' 'Yes, I do,' was the reply. Mencius added, 'Is the whiteness of a white feather like that of white snow, and the whiteness of white snow like that of white jade?' Kâo again said 'Yes.'

3. 'Very well,' pursued Mencius. 'Is the nature of a dog like the nature of an ox, and the nature of an ox like the nature of a man?'

●

1. The philosopher Kâo said, 'To enjoy food and delight in colours is nature. Benevolence is internal and not external; righteousness is external and not internal.'

2. Mencius asked him, 'What is the ground of your saying that benevolence is internal and righteousness external?' He replied, 'There is a man older than I, and I give honour to his age. It is not that there is first in me a principle of such reverence to age. It is just as when there is a white man, and I consider him white; according as he is so externally to me. On this account, I pronounce of righteousness that it is external.'

3. Mencius said, 'There is no difference between our pronouncing a white horse to be white and our pronouncing a white man to be white. But is there no difference between the regard with which we acknowledge the age of an old horse and that with which we acknowledge the age of an old man? And what is it which is called righteousness?– the fact of a man's being old? or the fact of our giving honour to his age?'

4. Kâo said, 'There is my younger brother;– I love him. But the younger brother of a man of Ch'in I do not love: that is, the feeling is determined by myself, and therefore I say that benevolence is internal. On the other hand, I give honour to an old man of Ch'û, and I also give honour to an old man of my own people: that is, the feeling is determined by the age, and therefore I say that righteousness is external.'

5. Mencius answered him, 'Our enjoyment of meat roasted by a man of Ch'in does not differ from our enjoyment of meat roasted by ourselves. Thus, what you insist on takes place also in the case of such things, and will you say likewise that our enjoyment of a roast is external?'

●

1. The disciple Mang Chî asked Kung-tû, saying, 'On what ground is it said that righteousness is internal?'

2. Kung-tû replied, 'We therein act out our feeling of respect, and therefore it is said to be internal.'

3. The other objected, 'Suppose the case of a villager older than your elder brother by one year, to which of them would you show the greater respect?' 'To my brother,' was the reply. 'But for which of them would you first pour out wine at a feast?' 'For the villager.' Mang Chî argued, 'Now your feeling of reverence rests on the one, and now the honour due to age is rendered to the other;– this is certainly determined by what is without, and does not proceed from within.'

4. Kung-tû was unable to reply, and told the conversation to Mencius. Mencius said, 'You should ask him, "Which do you respect most,– your uncle,

or your younger brother?" He will answer, "My uncle." Ask him again, "If your younger brother be personating a dead ancestor, to which do you show the greater respect,– to him or to your uncle?" He will say, "To my younger brother." You can go on, "But where is the respect due, as you said, to your uncle?" He will reply to this, "I show the respect to my younger brother, because of the position which he occupies," and you can likewise say, "So my respect to the villager is because of the position which he occupies. Ordinarily, my respect is rendered to my elder brother; for a brief season, on occasion, it is rendered to the villager."'

5. Mang Chî heard this and observed, 'When respect is due to my uncle, I respect him, and when respect is due to my younger brother, I respect him;– the thing is certainly determined by what is without, and does not proceed from within.' Kung-tû replied, 'In winter we drink things hot, in summer we drink things cold; and so, on your principle, eating and drinking also depend on what is external!'

•

1. The disciple Kung-tû said, 'The philosopher Kâo says, "Man's nature is neither good nor bad."

2. 'Some say, "Man's nature may be made to practise good, and it may be made to practise evil, and accordingly, under Wan and Wû, the people loved what was good, while under Yû and Lî, they loved what was cruel."

3. 'Some say, "The nature of some is good, and the nature of others is bad. Hence it was that under such a sovereign as Yâo there yet appeared Hsiang; that with such a father as Kû-sâu there yet appeared Shun; and that with Châu for their sovereign, and the son of their elder brother besides, there were found Ch'î, the viscount of Wei, and the prince Pî-Kan.

4. 'And now you say, "The nature is good." Then are all those wrong?'

5. Mencius said, 'From the feelings proper to it, it is constituted for the practice of what is good. This is what I mean in saying that the nature is good.

6. 'If men do what is not good, the blame cannot be imputed to their natural powers.

7. 'The feeling of commiseration belongs to all men; so does that of shame and dislike; and that of reverence and respect; and that of approving and disapproving. The feeling of commiseration implies the principle of benevolence; that of shame and dislike, the principle of righteousness; that of reverence and respect, the principle of propriety; and that of approving and disapproving, the principle of knowledge. Benevolence, righteousness, propriety, and knowledge are not infused into us from without. We are certainly furnished with them. And a different view is simply owing to want of reflection. Hence it is said, "Seek and you will find

them. Neglect and you will lose them." Men differ from one another in regard to them;– some as much again as others, some five times as much, and some to an incalculable amount:– it is because they cannot carry out fully their natural powers.

8. 'It is said in the Book of Poetry,

> *Heaven in producing mankind,*
> *Gave them their various faculties and relations with their specific laws.*
> *These are the invariable rules of nature for all to hold,*
> *And all love this admirable virtue.*

Confucius said, "The maker of this ode knew indeed the principle of our nature!" We may thus see that every faculty and relation must have its law, and since there are invariable rules for all to hold, they consequently love this admirable virtue.'

•

1. Mencius said, 'In good years the children of the people are most of them good, while in bad years the most of them abandon themselves to evil. It is not owing to any difference of their natural powers conferred by Heaven that they are thus different. The abandonment is owing to the circumstances through which they allow their minds to be ensnared and drowned in evil.

2. 'There now is barley.– Let it be sown and covered up; the ground being the same, and the time of sowing likewise the same, it grows rapidly up, and, when the full time is come, it is all found to be ripe. Although there may be inequalities of produce, that is owing to the difference of the soil, as rich or poor, to the unequal nourishment afforded by the rains and dews, and to the different ways in which man has performed his business in reference to it.

3. 'Thus all things which are the same in kind are like to one another;– why should we doubt in regard to man, as if he were a solitary exception to this? The sage and we are the same in kind.

4. 'In accordance with this the scholar Lung said, "If a man make hempen sandals without knowing the size of people's feet, yet I know that he will not make them like baskets." Sandals are all like one another, because all men's feet are like one another.

5. 'So with the mouth and flavours;– all mouths have the same relishes. Yî-yâ only apprehended before me what my mouth relishes. Suppose that his mouth in its relish for flavours differed from that of other men, as is the case with dogs or horses which are not the same in kind with us, why should all men be found following Yî-yâ in their relishes? In the matter of tastes all the people model themselves after Yî-yâ; that is, the mouths of all men are like one another.

6. 'And so also it is with the ear. In the matter of sounds, the whole people model themselves after the music-master K'wang; that is, the ears of all men are like one another.

7. 'And so also it is with the eye. In the case of Tsze-tû, there is no man but would recognise that he was beautiful. Any one who would not recognise the beauty of Tsze-tû must have no eyes.

8. 'Therefore I say,– Men's mouths agree in having the same relishes; their ears agree in enjoying the same sounds; their eyes agree in recognising the same beauty:– shall their minds alone be without that which they similarly approve? What is it then, of which they similarly approve? It is, I say, the principles of our nature, and the determinations of righteousness. The sages only apprehended before me that of which my mind approves along with other men. Therefore the principles of our nature and the determinations of righteousness are agreeable to my mind, just as the flesh of grass and grain-fed animals is agreeable to my mouth.'

•

1. Mencius said, 'The trees of the Niû mountain were once beautiful. Being situated, however, in the borders of a large State, they were hewn down with axes and bills;– and could they retain their beauty? Still through the activity of the vegetative life day and night, and the nourishing influence of the rain and dew, they were not without buds and sprouts springing forth, but then came the cattle and goats and browsed upon them. To these things is owing the bare and stripped appearance of the mountain, and when people now see it, they think it was never finely wooded. But is this the nature of the mountain?

2. 'And so also of what properly belongs to man;– shall it be said that the mind of any man was without benevolence and righteousness? The way in which a man loses his proper goodness of mind is like the way in which the trees are denuded by axes and bills. Hewn down day after day, can it– the mind– retain its beauty? But there is a development of its life day and night, and in the calm air of the morning, just between night and day, the mind feels in a degree those desires and aversions which are proper to humanity, but the feeling is not strong, and it is fettered and destroyed by what takes place during the day. This fettering taking place again and again, the restorative influence of the night is not sufficient to preserve the proper goodness of the mind; and when this proves insufficient for that purpose, the nature becomes not much different from that of the irrational animals, and when people now see it, they think that it never had those powers which I assert. But does this condition represent the feelings proper to humanity?

3. 'Therefore, if it receive its proper nourishment, there is nothing which will not grow. If it lose its proper nourishment, there is nothing which will not decay away.

4. 'Confucius said, "Hold it fast, and it remains with you. Let it go, and you lose it. Its outgoing and incoming cannot be defined as to time or place." It is the mind of which this is said!'

CHAPTER 22

1. Mencius said, 'It is not to be wondered at that the king is not wise!

2. 'Suppose the case of the most easily growing thing in the world;– if you let it have one day's genial heat, and then expose it for ten days to cold, it will not be able to grow. It is but seldom that I have an audience of the king, and when I retire, there come all those who act upon him like the cold. Though I succeed in bringing out some buds of goodness, of what avail is it?

3. 'Now chess-playing is but a small art, but without his whole mind being given, and his will bent, to it, a man cannot succeed at it. Chess Ch'iû is the best chess-player in all the kingdom. Suppose that he is teaching two men to play.– The one gives to the subject his whole mind and bends to it all his will, doing nothing but listening to Chess Ch'iû. The other, although he seems to be listening to him, has his whole mind running on a swan which he thinks is approaching, and wishes to bend his bow, adjust the string to the arrow, and shoot it. Although he is learning along with the other, he does not come up to him. Why?– because his intelligence is not equal? Not so.'

●

1. Mencius said, 'I like fish, and I also like bear's paws. If I cannot have the two together, I will let the fish go, and take the bear's paws. So, I like life, and I also like righteousness. If I cannot keep the two together, I will let life go, and choose righteousness.

2. 'I like life indeed, but there is that which I like more than life, and therefore, I will not seek to possess it by any improper ways. I dislike death indeed, but there is that which I dislike more than death, and therefore there are occasions when I will not avoid danger.

3. 'If among the things which man likes there were nothing which he liked more than life, why should he not use every means by which he could preserve it? If among the things which man dislikes there were nothing which he disliked more than death, why should he not do everything by which he could avoid danger?

4. 'There are cases when men by a certain course might preserve life, and they do not employ it; when by certain things they might avoid danger, and they will not do them.

5. 'Therefore, men have that which they like more than life, and that which they dislike more than death. They are not men of distinguished talents and virtue only who have this mental nature. All men have it; what belongs to such men is simply that they do not lose it.

6. 'Here are a small basket of rice and a platter of soup, and the case is one in which the getting them will preserve life, and the want of them will be death;– if they are offered with an insulting voice, even a tramper will not receive them, or if you first tread upon them, even a beggar will not stoop to take them.

7. 'And yet a man will accept of ten thousand chung, without any consideration of propriety or righteousness. What can the ten thousand chung add to him? When he takes them, is it not that he may obtain beautiful mansions, that he may secure the services of wives and concubines, or that the poor and needy of his acquaintance may be helped by him?

8. 'In the former case the offered bounty was not received, though it would have saved from death, and now the emolument is taken for the sake of beautiful mansions. The bounty that would have preserved from death was not received, and the emolument is taken to get the service of wives and concubines. The bounty that would have saved from death was not received, and the emolument is taken that one's poor and needy acquaintance may be helped by him. Was it then not possible likewise to decline this? This is a case of what is called– "Losing the proper nature of one's mind."'

•

1. Mencius said, 'Benevolence is man's mind, and righteousness is man's path.

2. 'How lamentable is it to neglect the path and not pursue it, to lose this mind and not know to seek it again!

3. 'When men's fowls and dogs are lost, they know to seek for them again, but they lose their mind, and do not know to seek for it.

4. 'The great end of learning is nothing else but to seek for the lost mind.'

•

1. Mencius said, 'Here is a man whose fourth finger is bent and cannot be stretched out straight. It is not painful, nor does it incommode his business, and yet if there be any one who can make it straight, he will not think the way from Ch'in to Ch'û far to go to him; because his finger is not like the finger of other people.

2. 'When a man's finger is not like those of other people, he knows to feel dissatisfied, but if his mind be not like that of other people, he does not know to feel dissatisfaction. This is called– "Ignorance of the relative importance of things."'

Mencius said, 'Anybody who wishes to cultivate the t'ung or the tsze, which may be grasped with both hands, perhaps with one, knows by what means to nourish them. In the case of their own persons, men do not know by what means to nourish them. Is it to be supposed that their regard of their own persons is inferior to their regard for a t'ung or tsze? Their want of reflection is extreme.'

•

1. Mencius said, 'There is no part of himself which a man does not love, and as he loves all, so he must nourish all. There is not an inch of skin which he does not love, and so there is not an inch of skin which he will not nourish. For examining whether his way of nourishing be good or not, what other rule is there but this, that he determine by reflecting on himself where it should be applied?

2. 'Some parts of the body are noble, and some ignoble; some great, and some small. The great must not be injured for the small, nor the noble for the ignoble. He who nourishes the little belonging to him is a little man, and he who nourishes the great is a great man.

3. 'Here is a plantation-keeper, who neglects his wû and chiâ, and cultivates his sour jujube-trees;– he is a poor plantation-keeper.

4. 'He who nourishes one of his fingers, neglecting his shoulders or his back, without knowing that he is doing so, is a man who resembles a hurried wolf.

5. 'A man who only eats and drinks is counted mean by others;– because he nourishes what is little to the neglect of what is great.

6. 'If a man, fond of his eating and drinking, were not to neglect what is of more importance, how should his mouth and belly be considered as no more than an inch of skin?'

•

1. The disciple Kung-tû said, 'All are equally men, but some are great men, and some are little men;– how is this?' Mencius replied, 'Those who follow that part of themselves which is great are great men; those who follow that part which is little are little men.'

2. Kung-tû pursued, 'All are equally men, but some follow that part of themselves which is great, and some follow that part which is little;– how is this?' Mencius answered, 'The senses of hearing and seeing do not think, and are obscured by external things. When one thing comes into contact with another, as a matter of course it leads it away. To the mind belongs the office of thinking. By thinking, it gets the right view of things; by neglecting to think, it fails to do this. These – the senses and the mind – are what Heaven has given to us. Let a man first stand fast in the supremacy of the nobler part of his constitution, and the inferior part will not be able to take it from him. It is simply this which makes the great man.'

•

1. Mencius said, 'There is a nobility of Heaven, and there is a nobility of man. Benevolence, righteousness, self-consecration, and fidelity, with unwearied joy in these virtues;– these constitute the nobility of Heaven. To be a kung, a ch'ing, or a tâ-fû;– this constitutes the nobility of man.

2. 'The men of antiquity cultivated their nobility of Heaven, and the nobility of man came to them in its train.

3. 'The men of the present day cultivate their nobility of Heaven in order to seek for the nobility of man, and when they have obtained that, they throw away the other:– their delusion is extreme. The issue is simply this, that they must lose that nobility of man as well.'

•

1. Mencius said, 'To desire to be honoured is the common mind of men. And all men have within themselves that which is truly honourable. Only they do not think of it.

2. 'The honour which men confer is not good honour. Those whom Châo the Great ennobles he can make mean again.

3. 'It is said in the Book of Poetry,

He has filled us with his wine,
He has satiated us with his goodness.

"Satiated us with his goodness," that is, satiated us with benevolence and righteousness, and he who is so satiated, consequently, does not wish for the fat meat and fine millet of men. A good reputation and far-reaching praise fall to him, and he does not desire the elegant embroidered garments of men.'

•

1. Mencius said, 'Benevolence subdues its opposite just as water subdues fire. Those, however, who now-a-days practise benevolence do it as if with one cup of water they could save a whole waggon-load of fuel which was on fire, and when the flames were not extinguished, were to say that water cannot subdue fire. This conduct, moreover, greatly encourages those who are not benevolent.

2. 'The final issue will simply be this– the loss of that small amount of benevolence.'

•

Mencius said, 'Of all the seeds the best are the five kinds of grain, yet if they be not ripe, they are not equal to the t'e or the pae. So the value of benevolence depends entirely on it being brought to maturity.'

•

1. Mencius said,' Hou Yi, in teaching men to shoot, made it a rule to draw the bow to the full, and his pupils also did the same

2. 'A master-workman, in teaching others, uses the compass and square, and his pupils do the same.'

CHAPTER 23

1. A man of Zan asked the disciple Wû-lû, saying, 'Is an observance of the rules of propriety in regard to eating, or eating merely, the more important?' The answer was, 'The observance of the rules of propriety is the more important.'

2. 'Is the gratifying the appetite of sex, or the doing so only according to the rules of propriety, the more important?' The answer again was, 'The observance of the rules of propriety in the matter is the more important.'

3. The man pursued, 'If the result of eating only according to the rules of propriety will be death by starvation, while by disregarding those rules we may get food, must they still be observed in such a case? If according to the rule that he shall go in person to meet his wife a man cannot get married, while by disregarding that rule he may get married, must he still observe the rule in such a case?'

4. Wû-lû was unable to reply to these questions, and the next day he went to Tsâu, and told them to Mencius. Mencius said, 'What difficulty is there in answering these inquiries?'

5. 'If you do not adjust them at their lower extremities, but only put their tops on a level, a piece of wood an inch square may be made to be higher than the pointed peak of a high building.

6. 'Gold is heavier than feathers;– but does that saying have reference, on the one hand, to a single clasp of gold, and, on the other, to a waggon-load of feathers?

7. 'If you take a case where the eating is of the utmost importance and the observing the rules of propriety is of little importance, and compare the things together, why stop with saying merely that the eating is more important? So, taking the case where the gratifying the appetite of sex is of the utmost importance and the observing the rules of propriety is of little importance, why stop with merely saying that the gratifying the appetite is the more important?

8. 'Go and answer him thus, "If, by twisting your elder brother's arm, and snatching from him what he is eating, you can get food for yourself, while, if you do not do so, you will not get anything to eat, will you so twist his arm ? If by getting over your neighbour's wall, and dragging away his virgin daughter, you can get a wife, while if you do not do so, you will not be able to get a wife, will you so drag her away?"'

•

1. Chiâo of Tsâo asked Mencius, saying, 'It is said, "All men may be Yâos and Shuns;"– is it so?' Mencius replied, It is.'

2. Chiâo went on, 'I have heard that king Wan was ten cubits high, and T'ang nine. Now I am nine cubits four inches in height. But I can do nothing but eat my millet. What am I to do to realize that saying?'

3. Mencius answered him, 'What has this – the question of size – to do with the matter? It all lies simply in acting as such. Here is a man, whose strength was not equal to lift a duckling:– he was then a man of no strength. But to-day he says, "I can lift 3,000 catties' weight," and he is a man of strength. And so, he who can lift the weight which Wû Hwo lifted is just another Wû Hwo. Why should a man make a want of ability the subject of his grief? It is only that he will not do the thing.

4. 'To walk slowly, keeping behind his elders, is to perform the part of a younger. To walk quickly and precede his elders, is to violate the duty of a younger brother. Now, is it what a man cannot do – to walk slowly? It is what he does not do. The course of Yâo and Shun was simply that of filial piety and fraternal duty.

5. 'Wear the clothes of Yâo, repeat the words of Yâo, and do the actions of Yâo, and you will just be a Yâo. And, if you wear the clothes of Chieh, repeat the words of Chieh, and do the actions of Chieh, you will just be a Chieh.'

6. Chiâo said, 'I shall be having an interview with the prince of Tsâu, and can ask him to let me have a house to lodge in. I wish to remain here, and receive instruction at your gate.'

7. Mencius replied, 'The way of truth is like a great road. It is not difficult to know it. The evil is only that men will not seek it. Do you go home and search for it, and you will have abundance of teachers.'

•

1. Kung-sun Ch'âu asked about an opinion of the scholar Kâo, saying, 'Kâo observed, "The Hsiâo P'ân is the ode of a little man."' Mencius asked, 'Why did he say so?' 'Because of the murmuring which it expresses,' was the reply.

2. Mencius answered, 'How stupid was that old Kâo in dealing with the ode! There is a man here, and a native of Yüeh bends his bow to shoot him. I will advise him not to do so, but speaking calmly and smilingly;– for no other reason but that he is not related to me. But if my own brother be bending his bow to shoot the man, then I will advise him not to do so, weeping and crying the while;– for no other reason than that he is related to me. The dissatisfaction expressed in the Hsiâo P'ân is the working of relative affection, and that affection shows benevolence. Stupid indeed was old Kâo's criticism on the ode.'

3. Ch'âu then said, 'How is it that there is no dissatisfaction expressed in the K'âi Fang?'

4. Mencius replied, 'The parent's fault referred to in the K'âi Fang is small; that referred to in the Hsiâo P'ân is great. Where the parent's fault was great, not to have murmured on account of it would have increased the want of natural affection. Where the parent's fault was small, to have murmured on account of it would have been to act like water which frets and foams about a stone that interrupts its course. To increase the want of natural affection would have been unfilial, and to fret and foam in such a manner would also have been unfilial.

5 'Confucius said, "Shun was indeed perfectly filial! And yet, when he was fifty, he was full of longing desire about his parents."'

•

1. Sung K'ang being about to go to Ch'û, Mencius met him in Shih-ch'iû.

2. 'Master, where are you going?' asked Mencius.

3. K'ang replied, 'I have heard that Ch'in and Ch'û are fighting together, and I am going to see the king of Ch'û and persuade him to cease hostilities. If he shall not be pleased with my advice, I shall go to see the king of Ch'in, and persuade him in the same way. Of the two kings I shall surely find that I can succeed with one of them.'

4. Mencius said, 'I will not venture to ask about the particulars, but I should like to hear the scope of your plan. What course will you take to try to persuade them?' K'ang answered, 'I will tell them how unprofitable their course is to them.' 'Master,' said Mencius, 'your aim is great, but your argument is not good.

5. 'If you, starting from the point of profit, offer your persuasive counsels to the kings of Ch'in and Ch'û, and if those kings are pleased with the consideration of profit so as to stop the movements of their armies, then all belonging to those armies will rejoice in the cessation of war, and find their pleasure in the pursuit of profit. Ministers will serve their sovereign for the profit of which they cherish the thought; sons will serve their fathers, and younger brothers will serve their elder brothers, from the same consideration:– and the issue will be, that, abandoning benevolence and righteousness, sovereign and minister, father and son, younger brother and elder, will carry on all their intercourse with this thought of profit cherished in their breasts. But never has there been such a state of society, without ruin being the result of it.

6. 'If you, starting from the ground of benevolence and righteousness, offer your counsels to the kings of Ch'in and Ch'û, and if those kings are pleased with the consideration of benevolence and righteousness so as to stop the

operations of their armies, then all belonging to those armies will rejoice in the stopping from war, and find their pleasure in benevolence and righteousness. Ministers will serve their sovereign, cherishing the principles of benevolence and righteousness; sons will serve their fathers, and younger brothers will serve their elder brothers, in the same way:– and so, sovereign and minister, father and son, elder brother and younger, abandoning the thought of profit, will cherish the principles of benevolence and righteousness, and carry on all their intercourse upon them. But never has there been such a state of society, without the State where it prevailed rising to the royal sway. Why must you use that word "profit."'

•

1. When Mencius was residing in Tsâu, the younger brother of the chief of Zan, who was guardian of Zan at the time, paid his respects to him by a present of silks, which Mencius received, not going to acknowledge it. When he was sojourning in P'ing-lû, Ch'û, who was prime minister of the State, sent him a similar present, which he received in the same way.

2. Subsequently, going from Tsâu to Zan, he visited the guardian; but when he went from Ping-lû to the capital of Ch'î, he did not visit the minister Ch'û. The disciple Wû-lû was glad, and said, 'I have got an opportunity to obtain some instruction.'

3. He asked accordingly, 'Master, when you went to Zan, you visited the chief's brother; and when you went to Ch'î, you did not visit Ch'û. Was it not because he is only the minister?'

4. Mencius replied, 'No. It is said in the Book of History, "In presenting an offering to a superior, most depends on the demonstrations of respect. If those demonstrations are not equal to the things offered, we say there is no offering, that is, there is no act of the will presenting the offering."

5. 'This is because the things so offered do not constitute an offering to a superior.'

6. Wû-lû was pleased, and when some one asked him what Mencius meant, he said, 'The younger of Zan could not go to Tsâu, but the minister Ch'û might have gone to P'ing-lû.'

•

1. Shun-yü K'wan said, 'He who makes fame and meritorious services his first objects, acts with a regard to others. He who makes them only secondary objects, acts with a regard to himself. You, master, were ranked among the three chief ministers of the State, but before your fame and services had reached either to the prince or the people, you have left your place. Is this indeed the way of the benevolent?'

2. Mencius replied, 'There was Po˘î;– he abode in an inferior situation, and would not, with his virtue, serve a degenerate prince. There was Î Yin;– he five times went to T'ang, and five times went to Chieh. There was Hûi of Liû-hsiâ;– he did not disdain to serve a vile prince, nor did he decline a small office. The courses pursued by those three worthies were different, but their aim was one. And what was their one aim? We must answer– "To be perfectly virtuous." And so it is simply after this that superior men strive. Why must they all pursue the same course?'

3. K'wan pursued, 'In the time of the duke Mû of Lû, the government was in the hands of Kung-î, while Tsze-liû and Tsze-sze were ministers. And yet, the dismemberment of Lû then increased exceedingly. Such was the case, a specimen how your men of virtue are of no advantage to a kingdom!'

4. Mencius said, 'The prince of Yü did not use Pâi-lî Hsi, and thereby lost his State. The duke Mû of Chin used him, and became chief of all the princes. Ruin is the consequence of not employing men of virtue and talents;– how can it rest with dismemberment merely?'

5. K'wan urged again, 'Formerly, when Wang P'âo dwelt on the Ch'î, the people on the west of the Yellow River all became skilful at singing in his abrupt manner. When Mien Ch'ü lived in Kâo-t'ang, the people in the parts of Ch'î on the west became skilful at singing in his prolonged manner. The wives of Hwa Châu and Ch'î Liang bewailed their husbands so skilfully, that they changed the manners of the State. When there is the gift within, it manifests itself without. I have never seen the man who could do the deeds of a worthy, and did not realize the work of one. Therefore there are now no men of talents and virtue. If there were, I should know them.'

6. Mencius answered, 'When Confucius was chief minister of Justice in Lû, the prince came not to follow his counsels. Soon after there was the solstitial sacrifice, and when a part of the flesh presented in sacrifice was not sent to him, he went away even without taking off his cap of ceremony. Those who did not know him supposed it was on account of the flesh. Those who knew him supposed that it was on account of the neglect of the usual ceremony. The fact was, that Confucius wanted to go away on occasion of some small offence, not wishing to do so without some apparent cause. All men cannot be expected to understand the conduct of a superior man.'

CHAPTER 24

1. Mencius said, 'The five chiefs of the princes were sinners against the three kings. The princes of the present day are sinners against the five chiefs. The Great officers of the present day are sinners against the princes.

2. 'The sovereign visited the princes, which was called "A tour of Inspection." The princes attended at the court of the sovereign, which was called "Giving a report of office." It was a custom in the spring to examine the ploughing, and supply any deficiency of seed; and in autumn to examine the reaping, and assist where there was a deficiency of the crop. When the sovereign entered the boundaries of a State, if the new ground was being reclaimed, and the old fields well cultivated; if the old were nourished and the worthy honoured; and if men of distinguished talents were placed in office: then the prince was rewarded,– rewarded with an addition to his territory. On the other hand, if, on entering a State, the ground was found left wild or overrun with weeds; if the old were neglected and the worthy unhonoured; and if the offices were filled with hard tax-gatherers: then the prince was reprimanded. If a prince once omitted his attendance at court, he was punished by degradation of rank; if he did so a second time, he was deprived of a portion of his territory; if he did so a third time, the royal forces were set in motion, and he was removed from his government. Thus the sovereign commanded the punishment, but did not himself inflict it, while the princes inflicted the punishment, but did not command it. The five chiefs, however, dragged the princes to punish other princes, and hence I say that they were sinners against the three kings.

3. 'Of the five chiefs the most powerful was the duke Hwan. At the assembly of the princes in K'wei-ch'iû, he bound the victim and placed the writing upon it, but did not slay it to smear their mouths with the blood. The first injunction in their agreement was,– "Slay the unfilial; change not the son who has been appointed heir; exalt not a concubine to be the wife." The second was,– "Honour the worthy, and maintain the talented, to give distinction to the virtuous." The third was,– "Respect the old, and be kind to the young. Be not forgetful of strangers and travellers." The fourth was, "Let not offices be hereditary, nor let officers be pluralists. In the selection of officers let the object be to get the proper men. Let not a ruler take it on himself to put to death a Great officer." The fifth was,– "Follow no crooked policy in making embankments. Impose no restrictions on the sale of grain. Let there be no promotions without first announcing them to the sovereign." It was then said, "All we who have united in

this agreement shall hereafter maintain amicable relations." The princes of the present day all violate these five prohibitions, and therefore I say that the princes of the present day are sinners against the five chiefs.

4. 'The crime of him who connives at, and aids, the wickedness of his prince is small, but the crime of him who anticipates and excites that wickedness is great. The officers of the present day all go to meet their sovereigns' wickedness, and therefore I say that the Great officers of the present day are sinners against the princes.'

•

1. The prince of Lû wanted to make the minister Shan commander of his army.

2. Mencius said, 'To employ an uninstructed people in war may be said to be destroying the people. A destroyer of the people would not have been tolerated in the times of Yâo and Shun.

3. 'Though by a single battle you should subdue Ch'î, and get possession of Nan-yang, the thing ought not to be done.'

4. Shan changed countenance, and said in displeasure, 'This is what I, Kû-Lî, do not understand.'

5. Mencius said, 'I will lay the case plainly before you. The territory appropriated to the sovereign is 1,000 lî square. Without a thousand lî, he would not have sufficient for his entertainment of the princes. The territory appropriated to a Hâu is 100 lî square. Without 100 lî, he would not have sufficient wherewith to observe the statutes kept in his ancestral temple.

6. 'When Châu-kung was invested with the principalily of Lû, it was a hundred lî square. The territory was indeed enough, but it was not more than 100 lî. When T'âi-kung was invested with the principality of Ch'î, it was 100 lî square. The territory was indeed enough, but it was not more than 100 lî.

7. 'Now Lû is five times 100 lî square. If a true royal ruler were to arise, whether do you think that Lû would be diminished or increased by him?

8. 'If it were merely taking the place from the one State to give it to the other, a benevolent man would not do it;– how much less will he do so, when the end is to be sought by the slaughter of men!

9. 'The way in which a superior man serves his prince contemplates simply the leading him in the right path, and directing his mind to benevolence.'

•

1. Mencius said, 'Those who now-a-days serve their sovereigns say, "We can for our sovereign enlarge the limits of the cultivated ground, and fill his

treasuries and arsenals." Such persons are now-a-days called "Good ministers," but anciently they were called "Robbers of the people." If a sovereign follows not the right way, nor has his mind bent on benevolence, to seek to enrich him is to enrich a Chieh.

2. 'Or they will say, "We can for our sovereign form alliances with other States, so that our battles must be successful." Such persons are now-a-days called "Good ministers," but anciently they were called "Robbers of the people." If a sovereign follows not the right way, nor has his mind directed to benevolence, to seek to enrich him is to enrich a Chieh.

3. 'Although a prince, pursuing the path of the present day, and not changing its practices, were to have the throne given to him, he could not retain it for a single morning.'

•

1. Pâi Kwei said, 'I want to take a twentieth of the produce only as the tax. What do you think of it?'

2. Mencius said, 'Your way would be that of the Mo.

3. 'In a country of ten thousand families, would it do to have only one potter?' Kwei replied, 'No. The vessels would not be enough to use.'

4. Mencius went on, 'In Mo all the five kinds of grain are not grown; it only produces the millet. There are no fortified cities, no edifices, no ancestral temples, no ceremonies of sacrifice; there are no princes requiring presents and entertainments; there is no system of officers with their various subordinates. On these accounts a tax of one-twentieth of the produce is sufficient there.

5. 'But now it is the Middle Kingdom that we live in. To banish the relationships of men, and have no superior men;– how can such a state of things be thought of?

6. 'With but few potters a kingdom cannot subsist;– how much less can it subsist without men of a higher rank than others?

7. 'If we wish to make the taxation lighter than the system of Yâo and Shun, we shall just have a great Mo and a small Mo. If we wish to make it heavier, we shall just have the great Chieh and the small Chieh.'

•

1. Pâi Kwei said, 'My management of the waters is superior to that of Yü.'

2. Mencius replied, 'You are wrong, Sir. Yü's regulation of the waters was according to the laws of water.

3. 'He therefore made the four seas their receptacle, while you make the neighbouring States their receptacle.

4. 'Water flowing out of its channels is called an inundation. Inundating waters are a vast waste of water, and what a benevolent man detests. You are wrong, my good Sir.'

•

Mencius said, 'If a scholar have not faith, how shall he take a firm hold of things?'

•

1. The prince of Lû wanting to commit the administration of his government to the disciple Yo-chang, Mencius said, 'When I heard of it, I was so glad that I could not sleep.'

2. Kung-sun Ch'âu asked, 'Is Yo-chang a man of vigour?' and was answered, 'No.' 'Is he wise in council?' 'No.' 'Is he possessed of much information?' 'No.'

3. 'What then made you so glad that you could not sleep?'

4. 'He is a man who loves what is good.'

5. 'Is the love of what is good sufficient?'

6. 'The love of what is good is more than a sufficient qualification for the government of the kingdom;– how much more is it so for the State of Lû!

7. 'If a minister love what is good, all within the four seas will count 1000 lî but a small distance, and will come and lay their good thoughts before him.

8. If he do not love what is good, men will say, "How self-conceited he looks? He is sayinq to himself, I know it." The language and looks of that self-conceit will keep men off at a distance of 1,000 lî. When good men stop 1,000 lî off, calumniators, flatterers, and sycophants will make their appearance. When a minister lives among calumniators, flatterers, and sycophants, though he may wish the State to be well governed, is it possible for it to be so?'

•

1. The disciple Ch'in said, 'What were the principles on which superior men of old took office?' Mencius replied, 'There were three cases in which they accepted office, and three in which they left it.'

2. 'If received with the utmost respect and all polite observances, and they could say to themselves that the prince would carry their words into practice, then they took office with him. Afterwards, although there might be no remission in the polite demeanour of the prince, if their words were not carried into practice, they would leave him.

3. 'The second case was that in which, though the prince could not be expected at once to carry their words into practice, yet being received by him with the utmost respect, they took office with him. But afterwards, if there was a remission in his polite demeanour, they would leave him.

4. 'The last case was that of the superior man who had nothing to eat, either morning or evening, and was so famished that he could not move out of his door. If the prince, on hearing of his state, said, "I must fail in the great point,– that of carrying his doctrines into practice, neither am I able to follow his words, but I am ashamed to allow him to die of want in my country;" the assistance offered in such a case might be received, but not beyond what was sufficient to avert death.'

•

1. Mencius said, 'Shun rose from among the channelled fields. Fû Yüeh was called to office from the midst of his building frames; Chiâo-ko from his fish and salt; Kwan Î-wû from the hands of his gaoler; Sun-shû Âo from his hiding by the sea-shore; and Pâi-lî Hsî from the market-place.

2. 'Thus, when Heaven is about to confer a great office on any man, it first exercises his mind with suffering, and his sinews and bones with toil. It exposes his body to hunger, and subjects him to extreme poverty. It confounds his undertakings. By all these methods it stimulates his mind, hardens his nature, and supplies his incompetencies.

3. 'Men for the most part err, and are afterwards able to reform. They are distressed in mind and perplexed in their thoughts, and then they arise to vigorous reformation. When things have been evidenced in men's looks, and set forth in their words, then they understand them.

4. 'If a prince have not about his court families attached to the laws and worthy counsellors, and if abroad there are not hostile States or other external calamities, his kingdom will generally come to ruin.

5. 'From these things we see how life springs from sorrow and calamity, and death from ease and pleasure.'

•

Mencius said, 'There are many arts in teaching. I refuse, as inconsistent with my character, to teach a man, but I am only thereby still teaching him.

CHAPTER 25

1. Mencius said, 'He who has exhausted all his mental constitution knows his nature. Knowing his nature, he knows Heaven.

2. 'To preserve one's mental constitution, and nourish one's nature, is the way to serve Heaven.

3. 'When neither a premature death nor long life causes a man any double-mindedness, but he waits in the cultivation of his personal character for whatever issue;– this is the way in which he establishes his Heaven-ordained being.'

•

1. Mencius said, 'There is an appointment for everything. A man should receive submissively what may be correctly ascribed thereto.

2. 'Therefore, he who has the true idea of what is Heaven's appointment will not stand beneath a precipitous wall.

3. 'Death sustained in the discharge of one's duties may correctly be ascribed to the appointment of Heaven.

4. 'Death under handcuffs and fetters cannot correctly be so ascribed.'

•

1. Mencius said, 'When we get by our seeking and lose by our neglecting;– in that case seeking is of use to getting, and the things sought for are those which are in ourselves.

2. 'When the seeking is according to the proper course, and the getting is only as appointed;– in that case the seeking is of no use to getting, and the things sought are without ourselves.'

•

1. Mencius said, 'All things are already complete in us.

2. 'There is no greater delight than to be conscious of sincerity on self-examination.

3. 'If one acts with a vigorous effort at the law of reciprocity, when he seeks for the realization of perfect virtue, nothing can be closer than his approximation to it.'

•

Mencius said, 'To act without understanding, and to do so habitually without examination, pursuing the proper path all life long, without knowing its true nature;– this is the way of multitudes.'

•

Mencius said, 'A man may not be without shame. When one is ashamed of having been without shame, he will afrwards not have occasion for shame.'

•

1. Mencius said, 'The sense of shame is to a man of great importance.'

2. 'Those who form contrivances and versatile schemes distinguished for their artfulness, do not allow their sense of shame to come into action.

3. 'When one differs from other men in not having this sense of shame, what will he have in common with them?'

•

Mencius said, 'The able and virtuous monarchs of antiquity loved virtue and forgot their power. And shall an exception be made of the able and virtuous scholars of antiquity, that they did not do the same? They delighted in their own principles, and were oblivious of the power of princes. Therefore, if kings and dukes did not show the utmost respect, and observe all forms of ceremony, they were not permitted to come frequently and visit them. If they thus found it not in their power to pay them frequent visits, how much less could they get to employ them as ministers?'

•

1. Mencius said to Sung Kâu-ch'ien, 'Are you fond, Sir, of travelling to the different courts? I will tell you about such travelling.

2. 'If a prince acknowledge you and follow your counsels, be perfectly satisfied. If no one do so, be the same.'

3. Kâu-ch'ien said, 'What is to be done to secure this perfect satisfaction?' Mencius replied, 'Honour virtue and delight in righteousness, and so you may always be perfectly satisfied.

4. 'Therefore, a scholar, though poor, does not let go his righteousness; though prosperous, he does not leave his own path.

5. 'Poor and not letting righteousness go;– it is thus that the scholar holds possession of himself. Prosperous and not leaving the proper path;– it is thus that the expectations of the people from him are not disappointed.

6. 'When the men of antiquity realized their wishes, benefits were conferred by them on the people. If they did not realize their wishes, they cultivated their personal character, and became illustrious in the world. If poor, they attended to their own virtue in solitude; if advanced to dignity, they made the whole kingdom virtuous as well.'

•

Mencius said, 'The mass of men wait for a king Wan, and then they will receive a rousing impulse. Scholars distinguished from the mass, without a king Wan, rouse themselves.'

•

Mencius said, 'Add to a man the families of Han and Wei. If he then look upon himself without being elated, he is far beyond the mass of men.'

•

Mencius said, 'Let the people be employed in the way which is intended to secure their ease, and though they be toiled, they will not murmur. Let them be put to death in the way which is intended to preserve their lives, and though they die, they will not murmur at him who puts them to death.'

•

1. Mencius said, 'Under a chief, leading all the princes, the people look brisk and cheerful. Under a true sovereign, they have an air of deep contentment.

2. 'Though he slay them, they do not murmur. When he benefits them, they do not think of his merit. From day to day they make progress towards what is good, without knowing who makes them do so.

3. 'Wherever the superior man passes through, transformation follows; wherever he abides, his influence is of a spiritual nature. It flows abroad, above and beneath, like that of Heaven and Earth. How can it be said that he mends society but in a small way!'

•

1. Mencius said, 'Kindly words do not enter so deeply into men as a reputation for kindness.

2. 'Good government does not lay hold of the people so much as good instructions.

3. 'Good government is feared by the people, while good instructions are loved by them. Good government gets the people's wealth, while good instructions get their hearts.'

•

1. Mencius said, 'The ability possessed by men without having been acquired by learning is intuitive ability, and the knowledge possessed by them without the exercise of thought is their intuitive knowledge.

2. 'Children carried in the arms all know to love their parents, and when they are grown a little, they all know to love their elder brothers.

3. 'Filial affection for parents is the working of benevolence. Respect

for elders is the working of righteousness. There is no other reason for those feelings;– they belong to all under heaven.'

•

Mencius said, 'When Shun was living amid the deep retired mountains, dwelling with the trees and rocks, and wandering among the deer and swine, the difference between him and the rude inhabitants of those remote hills appeared very small. But when he heard a single good word, or saw a single good action, he was like a stream or a river bursting its banks, and flowing out in an irresistible flood.'

•

Mencius said, 'Let a man not do what his own sense of righteousness tells him not to do, and let him not desire what his own sense of righteousness tells him not to desire;– to act thus is all he has to do.'

•

1. Mencius said, 'Men who are possessed of intelligent virtue and prudence in affairs will generally be found to have been in sickness and troubles.

2. 'They are the friendless minister and concubine's son, who keep their hearts under a sense of peril, and use deep precautions against calamity. On this account they become distinguished for their intelligence.'

•

1.Mencius said, 'There are persons who serve the prince;– they serve the prince, that is, for the sake of his countenance and favour.'

2. 'There are ministers who seek the tranquillity of the State, and find their pleasure in securing that tranquillity.

3. 'There are those who are the people of Heaven. They, judging that, if they were in office, they could carry out their principles, throughout the kingdom, proceed so to carry them out.

4. 'There are those who are great men. They rectify themselves and others are rectified.'

•

1. Mencius said, 'The superior man has three things in which he delights, and to be ruler over the empire is not one of them.'

2. 'That his father and mother are both alive, and that the condition of his brothers affords no cause for anxiety;– this is one delight.

3. 'That, when looking up, he has no occasion for shame before Heaven, and, below, he has no occasion to blush before men;– this is a second delight.

4. 'That he can get from the whole kingdom the most talented individuals, and teach and nourish them;– this is the third delight.

5. 'The superior man has three things in which he delights, and to be ruler over the kingdom is not one of them.'

•

1. Mencius said, 'Wide territory and a numerous people are desired by the superior man, but what he delights in is not here.

2. 'To stand in the centre of the kingdom, and tranquillize the people within the four seas;– the superior man delights in this, but the highest enjoyment of his nature is not here.

3. What belongs by his nature to the superior man cannot be increased by the largeness of his sphere of action, nor diminished by his dwelling in poverty and retirement;– for this reason, that it is determinately apportioned to him by Heaven.

4. 'What belongs by his nature to the superior man are benevolence, righteousness, propriety, and knowledge. These are rooted in his heart; their growth and manifestation are a mild harmony appearing in the countenance, a rich fullness in the back, and the character imparted to the four limbs. Those limbs understand to arrange themselves, without being told.'

•

1. Mencius said, 'Po-î, that he might avoid Châu, was dwelling on the coast of the northern sea when he heard of the rise of king Wan. He roused himself and said, "Why should I not go and follow him? I have heard that the chief of the West knows well how to nourish the old." T'âi-kung, to avoid Châu, was dwelling on the coast of the eastern sea. When he heard of the rise of king Wan, he said, "Why should I not go and follow him? I have heard that the chief of the West knows well how to nourish the old." If there were a prince in the kingdom, who knew well how to nourish the old, all men of virtue would feel that he was the proper object for them to gather to.

2. 'Around the homestead with its five mâu, the space beneath the walls was planted with mulberry trees, with which the women nourished silkworms, and thus the old were able to have silk to wear. Each family had five brood hens and two brood sows, which were kept to their breeding seasons, and thus the old were able to have flesh to eat. The husbandmen cultivated their farms of 100 mâu, and thus their families of eight mouths were secured against want.

3. 'The expression, "The chief of the West knows well how to nourish the old," refers to his regulation of the fields and dwellings, his teaching them to plant the mulberry and nourish those animals, and his instructing the wives

and children, so as to make them nourish their aged. At fifty, warmth cannot be maintained without silks, and at seventy flesh is necessary to satisfy the appetite. Persons not kept warm nor supplied with food are said to be starved and famished, but among the people of king Wan, there were no aged who were starved or famished. This is the meaning of the expression in question.'

•

1. Mencius said, 'Let it be seen to that their fields of grain and hemp are well cultivated, and make the taxes on them light;– so the people may be made rich.

2. 'Let it be seen to that the people use their resources of food seasonably, and expend their wealth only on the prescribed ceremonies:– so their wealth will be more than can be consumed.

3. 'The people cannot live without water and fire, yet if you knock at a man's door in the dusk of the evening, and ask for water and fire, there is no man who will not give them, such is the abundance of these things. A sage governs the kingdom so as to cause pulse and grain to be as abundant as water and fire. When pulse and grain are as abundant as water and fire, how shall the people be other than virtuous?'

CHAPTER 26

1. Mencius said, 'Confucius ascended the eastern hill, and Lû appeared to him small. He ascended the T'âi mountain, and all beneath the heavens appeared to him small. So he who has contemplated the sea, finds it difficult to think anything of other waters, and he who has wandered in the gate of the sage, finds it difficult to think anything of the words of others.

2. 'There is an art in the contemplation of water.– It is necessary to look at it as foaming in waves. The sun and moon being possessed of brilliancy, their light admitted even through an orifice illuminates.

3. 'Flowing water is a thing which does not proceed till it has filled the hollows in its course. The student who has set his mind on the doctrines of the sage, does not advance to them but by completing one lesson after another.'

•

1. Mencius said, 'He who rises at cock-crowing and addresses himself earnestly to the practice of virtue, is a disciple of Shun.

2. 'He who rises at cock-crowing, and addresses himself earnestly to the pursuit of gain, is a disciple of Chih.

3. 'If you want to know what separates Shun from Chih, it is simply this,– the interval between the thought of gain and the thought of virtue.'

•

1. Mencius said, 'The principle of the philosopher Yang was– "Each one for himself." Though he might have benefited the whole kingdom by plucking out a single hair, he would not have done it.

2. 'The philosopher Mo loves all equally. If by rubbing smooth his whole body from the crown to the heel, he could have benefited the kingdom, he would have done it.

3. 'Tsze-mo holds a medium between these. By holding that medium, he is nearer the right. But by holding it without leaving room for the exigency of circumstances, it becomes like their holding their one point.

4. 'The reason why I hate that holding to one point is the injury it does to the way of right principle. It takes up one point and disregards a hundred others.'

•

1. Mencius said, 'The hungry think any food sweet, and the thirsty think the same of any drink, and thus they do not get the right taste of what they eat and drink.

The hunger and thirst, in fact, injure their palate. And is it only the mouth and belly which are injured by hunger and thirst? Men's minds are also injured by them.

2. 'If a man can prevent the evils of hunger and thirst from being any evils to his mind, he need not have any sorrow about not being equal to other men.'

•

Mencius said, 'A man with definite aims to be accomplished may be compared to one digging a well. To dig the well to a depth of seventy-two cubits, and stop without reaching the spring, is after all throwing away the well.'

•

1. Mencius said, 'Benevolence and righteousness were natural to Yâo and Shun. T'ang and Wû made them their own. The five chiefs of the princes feigned them.

2. 'Having borrowed them long and not returned them, how could it be known they did not own them?'

•

1. Kung-sun Ch'âu said, 'Î Yin said, "I cannot be near and see him so disobedient to reason," and therewith he banished T'â-chiâ to T'ung. The people were much pleased. When T'â-chiâ became virtuous, he brought him back, and the people were again much pleased.

2. 'When worthies are ministers, may they indeed banish their sovereigns in this way when they are not virtuous?'

3. Mencius replied, 'If they have the same purpose as Î Yin, they may. If they have not the same purpose, it would be usurpation.'

•

1. Kung-sun Ch'âu said, 'It is said, in the Book of Poetry,

He will not eat the bread of idleness!

How is it that we see superior men eating without labouring?' Mencius replied, 'When a superior man resides in a country, if its sovereign employ his counsels, he comes to tranquillity, wealth and glory. If the young in it follow his instructions, they become filial, obedient to their elders, true-hearted, and faithful. What greater example can there be than this of not eating the bread of idleness?'

•

1. The king's son, Tien, asked Mencius, saying, 'What is the business of the unemployed scholar?'

2. Mencius replied, 'To exalt his aim.'

3. Tien asked again, 'What do you mean by exalting the aim?' The answer was, 'Setting it simply on benevolence and righteousness. He thinks how to put a single

innocent person to death is contrary to benevolence; how to take what one has not a right to is contrary to righteousness; that one's dwelling should be benevolence; and one's path should be righteousness. Where else should he dwell? What other path should he pursue? When benevolence is the dwelling-place of the heart, and righteousness the path of the life, the business of a great man is complete.'

•

Mencius said, 'Supposing that the kingdom of Ch'î were offered, contrary to righteousness, to Ch'an Chung, he would not receive it, and all people believe in him, as a man of the highest worth. But this is only the righteousness which declines a dish of rice or a plate of soup. A man can have no greater crimes than to disown his parents and relatives, and the relations of sovereign and minister, superiors and inferiors. How can it be allowed to give a man credit for the great excellences because he possesses a small one?'

•

1. T'âo Ying asked, saying, 'Shun being sovereign, and Kâo-yâo chief minister of justice, if Kû-sâu had murdered a man, what would have been done in the case?'

2. Mencius said, 'Kâo-yâo would simply have apprehended him.'

3. 'But would not Shun have forbidden such a thing?'

4. 'Indeed, how could Shun have forbidden it? Kâo-yâo had received the law from a proper source.'

5. 'In that case what would Shun have done?'

6. 'Shun would have regarded abandoning the kingdom as throwing away a worn-out sandal. He would privately have taken his father on his back, and retired into concealment, living some where along the sea-coast. There he would have been all his life, cheerful and happy, forgetting the kingdom.'

•

1. Mencius, going from Fan to Ch'î, saw the king of Ch'î's son at a distance, and said with a deep sigh, 'One's position alters the air, just as the nurture affects the body. Great is the influence of position! Are we not all men's sons in this respect?'

2. Mencius said, 'The residence, the carriages and horses, and the dress of the king's son, are mostly the same as those of other men. That he looks so is occasioned by his position. How much more should a peculiar air distinguish him whose position is in the wide house of the world!

3. 'When the prince of Lû went to Sung, he called out at the T'ieh-châi gate, and the keeper said, "This is not our prince. How is it that his voice is so like that of our prince?" This was occasioned by nothing but the correspondence of their positions.'

●

1. Mencius said, 'To feed a scholar and not love him, is to treat him as a pig. To love him and not respect him, is to keep him as a domestic animal.

2. 'Honouring and respecting are what exist before any offering of gifts.

3. 'If there be honouring and respecting without the reality of them, a superior man may not be retained by such empty demonstrations.'

●

Mencius said, 'The bodily organs with their functions belong to our Heaven-conferred nature. But a man must be a sage before he can satisfy the design of his bodily organization.'

●

1. The King Hsüan of Ch'î wanted to shorten the period of mourning. Kung-sun Ch'âu said, 'To have one whole year's mourning is better than doing away with it altogether.'

2. Mencius said, 'That is just as if there were one twisting the arm of his elder brother, and you were merely to say to him "Gently, gently, if you please." Your only course should be to teach such an one filial piety and fraternal duty.'

3. At that time, the mother of one of the king's sons had died, and his tutor asked for him that he might be allowed to observe a few months' mourning. Kung-sun Ch'âu asked, 'What do you say of this?'

4. Mencius replied, 'This is a case where the party wishes to complete the whole period, but finds it impossible to do so. The addition of even a single day is better than not mourning at all. I spoke of the case where there was no hindrance, and the party neglected the thing itself.'

●

1. Mencius said, 'There are five ways in which the superior man effects his teaching.

2. 'There are some on whom his influence descends like seasonable rain.

3. 'There are some whose virtue he perfects, and some of whose talents he assists the development.

4. 'There are some whose inquiries he answers.

5. 'There are some who privately cultivate and correct themselves.

6. These five ways are the methods in which the superior man effects his teaching.'

●

1. Kung-sun Ch'âu said, 'Lofty are your principles and admirable, but to learn them may well be likened to ascending the heavens,– something which cannot be reached. Why not adapt your teaching so as to cause learners to consider them attainable, and so daily exert themselves!'

2. Mencius said, 'A great artificer does not, for the sake of a stupid workman, alter or do away with the marking-line. Î did not, for the sake of a stupid archer, change his rule for drawing the bow.

3. 'The superior man draws the bow, but does not discharge the arrow, having seemed to leap with it to the mark; and he there stands exactly in the middle of the path. Those who are able, follow him.'

•

1. Mencius said, 'When right principles prevail throughout the kingdom, one's principles must appear along with one's person. When right principles disappear from the kingdom, one's person must vanish along with one's principles.

2. 'I have not heard of one's principles being dependent for their manifestation on other men.'

•

1. The disciple Kung-tû said, 'When Kang of T'ang made his appearance in your school, it seemed proper that a polite consideration should be paid to him, and yet you did not answer him. Why was that?'

2. Mencius replied, 'I do not answer him who questions me presuming on his nobility, nor him who presumes on his talents, nor him who presumes on his age, nor him who presumes on services performed to me, nor him who presumes on old acquaintance. Two of those things were chargeable on Kang of T'ang.'

•

1. Mencius said, 'He who stops short where stopping is acknowledged to be not allowable, will stop short in everything. He who behaves shabbily to those whom he ought to treat well, will behave shabbily to all.

2. 'He who advances with precipitation will retire with speed.'

•

Mencius said, 'In regard to inferior creatures, the superior man is kind to them, but not loving. In regard to people generally, he is loving to them, but not affectionate. He is affectionate to his parents, and lovingly disposed to people generally. He is lovingly disposed to people generally, and kind to creatures.'

•

1. Mencius said, 'The wise embrace all knowledge, but they are most earnest about what is of the greatest importance. The benevolent embrace all in their

love, but what they consider of the greatest importance is to cultivate an earnest affection for the virtuous. Even the wisdom of Yâo and Shun did not extend to everything, but they attended earnestly to what was important. Their benevolence did not show itself in acts of kindness to every man, but they earnestly cultivated an affection for the virtuous.

2. 'Not to be able to keep the three years' mourning, and to be very particular about that of three months, or that of five months; to eat immoderately and swill down the soup, and at the same time to inquire about the precept not to tear the meat with the teeth;– such things show what I call an ignorance of what is most important.'

CHAPTER 27

1. Mencius said, 'The opposite indeed of benevolent was the king Hûi of Liang! The benevolent, beginning with what they care for, proceed to what they do not care for. Those who are the opposite of benevolent, beginning with what they do not care for, proceed to what they care for.'

2. 'Kung-sun Ch'âu said, 'What do you mean?' Mencius answered, 'The king Hûi of Liang, for the matter of territory, tore and destroyed his people, leading them to battle. Sustaining a great defeat, he would engage again, and afraid lest they should not be able to secure the victory, urged his son whom he loved till he sacrificed him with them. This is what I call– "beginning with what they do not care for, and proceeding to what they care for."'

•

1. Mencius said, 'In the "Spring and Autumn" there are no righteous wars. Instances indeed there are of one war better than another.

2. '"Correction" is when the supreme authority punishes its subjects by force of arms. Hostile States do not correct one another.'

•

1. Mencius said, 'It would be better to be without the Book of History than to give entire credit to it.

2. 'In the "Completion of the War," I select two or three passages only, which I believe.

3. '"The benevolent man has no enemy under heaven. When the prince, the most benevolent, was engaged against him who was the most the opposite, how could the blood of the people have flowed till it floated the pestles of the mortars?"'

•

1. Mencius said, 'There are men who say– "I am skilful at marshalling troops, I am skilful at conducting a battle!"– They are great criminals.

2. 'If the ruler of a State love benevolence, he will have no enemy in the kingdom.

3. When T'ang was executing his work of correction in the south, the rude tribes on the north murmured. When he was executing it in the east, the rude tribes on the west murmured. Their cry was– "Why does he make us last?"

4. 'When king Wû punished Yin, he had only three hundred chariots of war, and three thousand life-guards.

5. 'The king said, "Do not fear. Let me give you repose. I am no enemy to the people!" On this, they bowed their heads to the earth, like the horns of animals falling off.

6. '"Royal correction" is but another word for rectifying. Each State wishing itself to be corrected, what need is there for fighting?'

•

Mencius said, 'A carpenter or a carriage-maker may give a man the circle and square, but cannot make him skilful in the use of them.'

•

Mencius said, 'Shun's manner of eating his parched grain and herbs was as if he were to be doing so all his life. When he became sovereign, and had the embroidered robes to wear, the lute to play, and the two daughters of Yâo to wait on him, he was as if those things belonged to him as a matter of course.'

•

Mencius said, 'From this time forth I know the heavy consequences of killing a man's near relations. When a man kills another's father, that other will kill his father; when a man kills another's elder brother, that other will kill his elder brother. So he does not himself indeed do the act, but there is only an interval between him and it.'

•

1. Mencius said, 'Anciently, the establishment of the frontier-gates was to guard against violence.

2. 'Nowadays, it is to exercise violence.'

•

Mencius said, 'If a man himself do not walk in the right path, it will not be walked in even by his wife and children. If he order men according to what is not the right way, he will not be able to get the obedience of even his wife and children.'

•

Mencius said, 'A bad year cannot prove the cause of death to him whose stores of gain are large; an age of corruption cannot confound him whose equipment of virtue is complete.'

•

Mencius said, 'A man who loves fame may be able to decline a State of a thousand chariots; but if he be not really the man to do such a thing, it will appear in his countenance, in the matter of a dish of rice or a platter of soup.'

•

1. Mencius said, 'If men of virtue and ability be not confided in, a State will become empty and void.

2. 'Without the rules of propriety and distinctions of right, the high and the low will be thrown into confusion.

3. 'Without the great principles of government and their various business, there will not be wealth sufficient for the expenditure.'

•

1. Mencius said, 'The people are the most important element in a nation; the spirits of the land and grain are the next; the sovereign is the lightest.

2. 'Therefore to gain the peasantry is the way to become sovereign; to gain the sovereign is the way to become a prince of a State; to gain the prince of a State is the way to become a great officer.

3. 'When a prince endangers the altars of the spirits of the land and grain, he is changed, and another appointed in his place.

4. 'When the sacrificial victims have been perfect, the millet in its vessels all pure, and the sacrifices offered at their proper seasons, if yet there ensue drought, or the waters overflow, the spirits of the land and grain are changed, and others appointed in their place.'

•

Mencius said, 'A sage is the teacher of a hundred generations:– this is true of Po-î and Hûi of Liû-Hsiâ. Therefore when men now bear the character of Po-î, the corrupt become pure, and the weak acquire determination. When they hear the character of Hûi of Liû-Hsiâ, the mean become generous, and the niggardly become liberal. Those two made themselves distinguished a hundred generations ago, and after a hundred generations, those who hear of them, are all aroused in this manner. Could such effects be produced by them, if they had not been sages? And how much more did they affect those who were in contiguity with them, and felt their inspiring influence!'

•

Mencius said, 'Benevolence is the distinguishing characteristic of man. As embodied in man's conduct, it is called the path of duty.

•

Mencius said, 'When Confucius was leaving Lû, he said, "I will set out by-and-by;"– this was the way in which to leave the State of his parents. When he was leaving Ch'î, he strained off with his hand the water in which his rice was being rinsed, took the rice, and went away;– this was the way in which to leave a strange State.'

•

Mencius said, 'The reason why the superior man was reduced to straits between Ch'an and Ts'âi was because neither the princes of the time nor their ministers sympathized or communicated with him.'

•

1. Mo Ch'î said, 'Greatly am I from anything to depend upon from the mouths of men.'

2. Mencius observed, 'There is no harm in that. Scholars are more exposed than others to suffer from the mouths of men.

3. 'It is said, in the Book of Poetry,

> *My heart is disquieted and grieved,*
> *I am hated by the crowd of mean creatures."*

This might have been said by Confucius. And again,

> *"Though he did not remove their wrath,*
> *He did not let fall his own fame."*

This might be said of king Wan.'

•

Mencius said, 'Anciently, men of virtue and talents by means of their own enlightenment made others enlightened. Nowadays, it is tried, while they are themselves in darkness, and by means of that darkness, to make others enlightened.'

•

Mencius said to the disciple Kâo, 'There are the footpaths along the hills;– if suddenly they be used, they become roads; and if, as suddenly they are not used, the wild grass fills them up. Now, the wild grass fills up your mind.'

•

1. The disciple Kâo said, 'The music of Yü was better than that of king Wan.'

2. Mencius observed, 'On what ground do you say so?' and the other replied, 'Because at the pivot the knob of Yü's bells is nearly worn through.'

3. Mencius said, 'How can that be a sufficient proof? Are the ruts at the gate of a city made by a single two-horsed chariot?'

•

1. When Ch'î was suffering from famine, Ch'an Tsin said to Mencius, 'The people are all thinking that you, Master, will again ask that the granary of T'ang be opened for them. I apprehend you will not do so a second time.'

2. Mencius said, 'To do it would be to act like Fang Fû. There was a man of that name in Tsin, famous for his skill in seizing tigers. Afterwards he became a scholar of reputation, and going once out to the wild country, he found the people all in pursuit of a tiger. The tiger took refuge in a corner of a hill, where no one dared to attack him, but when they saw Fang Fû, they ran and met him. Fang Fû immediately bared his arms, and descended from the carriage. The multitude were pleased with him, but those who were scholars laughed at him.'

CHAPTER 28

1. Mencius said, 'For the mouth to desire sweet tastes, the eye to desire beautiful colours, the ear to desire pleasant sounds, the nose to desire fragrant odours, and the four limbs to desire ease and rest;– these things are natural. But there is the appointment of Heaven in connexion with them, and the superior man does not say of his pursuit of them, "It is my nature."

2. 'The exercise of love between father and son, the observance of righteousness between sovereign and minister, the rules of ceremony between guest and host, the display of knowledge in recognising the talented, and the fulfilling the heavenly course by the sage;– these are the appointment of Heaven. But there is an adaptation of our nature for them. The superior man does not say, in reference to them, "It is the appointment of Heaven."'

●

1. Hâo-shang Pû-hâi asked, saying, 'What sort of man is Yo-chang?' Mencius replied, 'He is a good man, a real man.'

2. 'What do you mean by "A good man," "A real man?"'

3. The reply: 'A man who commands our liking is what is called a good man.

4. 'He whose goodness is part of himself is what is called real man.

5. 'He whose goodness has been filled up is what is called beautiful man.

6. 'He whose completed goodness is well displayed is what is called a great man.

7. 'When this great man exercises transforming influence, he is called a sage.

8. 'When the sage is beyond our knowledge, he is what is called a spirit-man.

9. 'Yo-chang is between the two first characters, and below the four last.'

●

1. Mencius said, 'Those who are fleeing from the errors of Mo naturally turn to Yang, and those who are fleeing from the errors of Yang naturally turn to orthodoxy. When they so turn, they should at once and simply be received.

2. 'Those who nowadays dispute with the followers of Yang and Mo do so as if they were pursuing a stray pig, the leg of which, after they have got it to enter the pen, they proceed to tie.'

●

Mencius said, 'There are the exactions of hempen-cloth and silk, of grain, and of personal service. The prince requires but one of these at once, deferring the other two. If he require two of them at once, then the people die of hunger. If he require the three at once, then fathers and sons are separated.'

Mencius said, 'The precious things of a prince are three;– the territory, the people, the government and its business. If one value as most precious pearls and jade, calamity is sure to befall him.'

●

Pan-ch'ang Kwo having obtained an official situation in Ch'î, Mencius said, 'He is a dead man, that Pan-ch'ang Kwo!' Pan-chang Kwo being put to death, the disciples asked, saying, 'How did you know, Master, that he would meet with death?' Mencius replied, 'He was a man, who had a little ability, but had not learned the great doctrines of the superior man. He was just qualified to bring death upon himself, but for nothing more.'

●

1. When Mencius went to T'ang, he was lodged in the Upper palace. A sandal in the process of making had been placed there in a window, and when the keeper of the place came to look for it, he could not find it.

2. On this, some one asked Mencius, saying, 'Is it thus that your followers pilfer?' Mencius replied, 'Do you think that they came here to pilfer the sandal?' The man said, 'I apprehend not. But you, Master, having arranged to give lessons, do not go back to inquire into the past, and you do not reject those who come to you. If they come with the mind to learn, you receive them without any more ado.'

●

1. Mencius said, 'All men have some things which they cannot bear;– extend that feeling to what they can bear, and benevolence will be the result. All men have some things which they will not do;– extend that feeling to the things which they do, and righteousness will be the result.

2. 'If a man can give full development to the feeling which makes him shrink from injuring others, his benevolence will be more than can be called into practice. If he can give full development to the feeling which refuses to break through, or jump over, a wall, his righteousness will be more than can be called into practice.

3. 'If he can give full development to the real feeling of dislike with which he receives the salutation, "Thou," "Thou," he will act righteously in all places and circumstances.

4. 'When a scholar speaks what he ought not to speak, by guile of speech seeking to gain some end; and when he does not speak what he ought to speak, by guile of silence seeking to gain some end;– both these cases are of a piece with breaking through a neighbour's wall.'

●

1. Mencius said, 'Words which are simple, while their meaning is far-reaching, are good words. Principles which, as held, are compendious, while

their application is extensive, are good principles. The words of the superior man do not go below the girdle, but great principles are contained in them.

2. 'The principle which the superior man holds is that of personal cultivation, but the kingdom is thereby tranquillized.

3. 'The disease of men is this:– that they neglect their own fields, and go to weed the fields of others, and that what they require from others is great, while what they lay upon themselves is light.'

•

1. Mencius said, 'Yâo and Shun were what they were by nature; T'ang and Wû were so by returning to natural virtue.

2. 'When all the movements, in the countenance and every turn of the body, are exactly what is proper, that shows the extreme degree of the complete virtue. Weeping for the dead should be from real sorrow, and not because of the living. The regular path of virtue is to be pursued without any bend, and from no view to emolument. The words should all be necessarily sincere, not with any desire to do what is right.

3. 'The superior man performs the law of right, and thereby waits simply for what has been appointed.'

•

1. Mencius said, 'Those who give counsel to the great should despise them, and not look at their pomp and display.

2. 'Halls several times eight cubits high, with beams projecting several cubits;– these, if my wishes were to be realized, I would not have. Food spread before me over ten cubits square, and attendants and concubines to the amount of hundreds;– these, though my wishes were realized, I would not have. Pleasure and wine, and the dash of hunting, with thousands of chariots following after me;– these, though my wishes were realized, I would not have. What they esteem are what I would have nothing to do with; what I esteem are the rules of the ancients.– Why should I stand in awe of them?'

•

Mencius said, 'To nourish the mind there is nothing better than to make the desires few. Here is a man whose desires are few:– in some things he may not be able to keep his heart, but they will be few. Here is a man whose desires are many:– in some things he may be able to keep his heart, but they will be few.'

•

1. Mencius said, 'Tsang Hsî was fond of sheep-dates, and his son, the philosopher Tsang, could not bear to eat sheep-dates.'

2. Kung-sun Ch'âu asked, saying, 'Which is best,– minced meat and broiled

meat, or sheep-dates?' Mencius said, 'Mince and broiled meat, to be sure.' Kung-sun Ch'âu went on, 'Then why did philosopher Tsang eat mince and broiled meat, and would not eat sheep-dates?' Mencius answered, 'For mince and broiled meat there is a common liking, while that for sheep-dates was peculiar. We avoid the name, but do not avoid the surname. The surname is common; the name is peculiar.'

•

1. Wan Chang asked, saying, 'Confucius, when he was in Ch'an, said: "Let me return. The scholars of my school are ambitious, but hasty. They are for advancing and seizing their object, but cannot forget their early ways." Why did Confucius, when he was in Ch'an, think of the ambitious scholars of Lû?'

2. Mencius replied, 'Confucius not getting men pursuing the true medium, to whom he might communicate his instructions, determined to take the ardent and the cautiously-decided. The ardent would advance to seize their object; the cautiously-decided would keep themselves from certain things. It is not to be thought that Confucius did not wish to get men pursuing the true medium, but being unable to assure himself of finding such, he therefore thought of the next class.'

3. 'I venture to ask what sort of men they were who could be styled "The ambitious?"'

4. 'Such,' replied Mencius, 'as Ch'in Chang, Tsang Hsî, and Mû P'ei, were those whom Confucius styled "ambitious."'

5. 'Why were they styled "ambitious?"'

6. The reply was, 'Their aim led them to talk magniloquently, saying, "The ancients!" "The ancients!" But their actions, where we fairly compare them with their words, did not correspond with them.

7. 'When he found also that he could not get such as were thus ambitious, he wanted to get scholars who would consider anything impure as beneath them. Those were the cautiously-decided, a class next to the former.'

8. Chang pursued his questioning, 'Confucius said, "They are only your good careful people of the villages at whom I feel no indignation, when they pass my door without entering my house. Your good careful people of the villages are the thieves of virtue." What sort of people were they who could be styled "Your good careful people of the villages?"'

9. Mencius replied, 'They are those who say, "Why are they so magniloquent? Their words have not respect to their actions and their actions have not respect to their words, but they say, "The ancients! The ancients! Why do they act so peculiarly, and are so cold and distant? Born in this age, we should be of this age, to be good is all that is needed." Eunuch-like, flattering their generation;– such are your good careful men of the villages.'

10. Wan Chang said, 'Their whole village styles those men good and careful. In all their conduct they are so. How was it that Confucius considered them the thieves of virtue?'

11. Mencius replied, 'If you would blame them, you find nothing to allege. If you would criticise them, you have nothing to criticise. They agree with the current customs. They consent with an impure age. Their principles have a semblance of right-heartedness and truth. Their conduct has a semblance of disinterestedness and purity. All men are pleased with them, and they think themselves right, so that it is impossible to proceed with them to the principles of Yâo and Shun. On this account they are called "The thieves of virtue."

12. 'Confucius said, "I hate a semblance which is not the reality. I hate the darnel, lest it be confounded with the corn. I hate glib-tonguedness, lest it be confounded with righteousness. I hate sharpness of tongue, lest it be confounded with sincerity. I hate the music of Chang, lest it be confounded with the true music. I hate the reddish blue, lest it be confounded with vermilion. I hate your good careful men of the villages, lest they be confounded with the truly virtuous."

13. 'The superior man seeks simply to bring back the unchanging standard, and, that being correct, the masses are roused to virtue. When they are so aroused, forthwith perversities and glossed wickedness disappear.'

●

1. Mencius said, 'From Yâo and Shun down to T'ang were 500 years and more. As to Yu and Kâo Yâo, they saw those earliest sages, and so knew their doctrines, while T'ang heard their doctrines as transmitted, and so knew them.

2. 'From T'ang to king Wan were 500 years and more. As to Î Yin, and Lâi Chû, they saw T'ang and knew his doctrines, while king Wan heard them as transmitted, and so knew them.

3. 'From king Wan to Confucius were 500 years and more. As to T'âi-kung Wang and San Î-shang, they saw Wan, and so knew his doctrines, while Confucius heard them as transmitted, and so knew them.

●

4. 'From Confucius downwards until now, there are only 100 years and somewhat more. The distance in time from the sage is so far from being remote, and so very near at hand was the sage's residence. In these circumstances, is there no one to transmit his doctrines? Yea, is there no one to do so?'

AZILOTH ||| BOOKS

Aziloth Books publishes a wide range of titles ranging from hard-to-find esoteric books - *Parchment Books* - to classic works on fiction, politics and philosophy - *Cathedral Classics*. Our newest venture is *Aziloth Books Children's Classics*, with vibrant new covers and illustrations to complement some of the world's very best children's tales. All our imprints are offered to the reader at a competitive price and through as many mediums and outlets as possible.

 We are committed to excellent book production and strive, whenever possible, to add value to our titles with original images, maps and author introductions. With the premium on space in most modern dwellings, we also endeavour - within the limits of good book design - to make our products as slender as possible, allowing more books to be fitted into a given bookshelf area.

We are a small, approachable company and would love to hear any of your comments and suggestions on our plans, products, or indeed on absolutely anything.

Aziloth Books, Rimey Law, Rookhope, Co. Durham, DL13 2BL, England.
t: 01388-517600 e: info@azilothbooks.com w: www.azilothbooks.com

PARCHMENT BOOKS enshrines the concept of the oneness of all true religious traditions - that "the light shines from many different lanterns". Our list below offers titles from both eastern and western spiritual traditions, including Christian, Judaic, Islamic, Daoist, Hindu and Buddhist mystical texts, as well as books on alchemy, hermeticism, paganism, etc..

By bringing together such spiritual texts, we hope to make esoteric and occult knowledge more readily available to those ready to receive it. We do not publish grimoires or titles pertaining to the left hand path. Titles include:

The Prophet	Khalil Gibran
The Madman: His Parables & Poems	Khalil Gibran
Abandonment to Divine Providence	Jean-Pierre de Caussade
Corpus Hermeticum	G. R. S. Mead (trans.)
The Holy Rule of St Benedict	St. Benedict of Nursia
The Confession of St Patrick	St. Patrick
The Outline of Sanity	G. K. Chesterton
An Outline of Occult Science	Rudolf Steiner
The Dialogue Of St Catherine Of Siena	St. Catherine of Siena
*Esoteric Christianity; Thought-Forms**	Annie Besant
The Teachings of Zoroaster	Shapurji A. Kapadia
The Spiritual Exercises of St. Ignatius	St. Ignatius of Loyola
Daemonologie	King James of England
A Dweller on Two Planets	Phylos the Thibetan
*Bushido**	Nitobe Inazo
The Interior Castle	St. Teresa of Avila
*Songs of Innocence & Experience**	William Blake
The Secret of the Rosary	St. Louis Marie de Montfort
From Ritual to Romance	Jessie L. Weston
The God of the Witches	Margaret Murray
Kundalini – an occult experience	George S. Arundale
The Kingdom of God is Within You	Leo Tolstoy
The Trial and Death of Socrates	Plato
A Textbook of Theosophy	Charles W. Leadbetter
Chuang Tzu: Daoist Teachings	Chuang Tzu
Practical Mysticism	Evelyn Underhill
Tao Te Ching (Lao Tzu's 'Book of the Way')	Tzu, Lao
The Most Holy Trinosophia	Le Comte de St.-Germain
Tertium Organum	P. D. Ouspensky
Totem and Taboo	Sigmund Freud
The Kebra Negast	E. A. Wallis Budge
Esoteric Buddhism	Alfred Percy Sinnett
Demian: the story of a youth	Hermann Hesse
Religio Medici	Thomas Browne
The Jefferson Bible	Thomas Jefferson
The Dhammapada	W.Wagiswara & K.Saunders
Magic & Mystery in Tibet	Alexandra David-Néel

* with colour illustrations
Obtainable at all good online and local bookstores.
View Aziloth Books' full list at: www.azilothbooks.com

CATHEDRAL CLASSICS hosts an array of classic literature, from erudite ancient tomes to avant-garde, twentieth-century masterpieces, all of which deserve a place in your home.   All the world's great novelists are here, Jane Austen, Dickens, Conrad, Arthur Machen and Henry James, brushing shoulders with such disparate luminaries as Sun Tzu, Marcus Aurelius, Kipling, Friedrich Nietzsche, Machiavelli, and Omar Khayam. A small selection is detailed below:

Frankenstein	Mary Shelley
Herland; With Her in Ourland	Charlotte Perkins Gilman
The Time Machine; The Invisible Man	H. G. Wells
Three Men in a Boat	Jerome K Jerome
The Rubaiyat of Omar Khayyam	Omar Khayyam
A Study in Scarlet	Arthur Conan Doyle
The Sign of the Four	Arthur Conan Doyle
The Picture of Dorian Gray	Oscar Wilde
Flatland	Edwin A. Abbott
The Coming Race	Bulwer Lytton
The Adventures of Sherlock Holmes	Arthur Conan Doyle
The Great God Pan	Arthur Machen
Beyond Good and Evil	Friedrich Nietzsche
England, My England	D. H. Lawrence
The Castle of Otranto	Horace Walpole
Self-Reliance, & Other Essays (series1&2)	Ralph W. Emmerson
The Art of War	Sun Tzu
A Shepherd's Life	W. H. Hudson
The Double	Fyodor Dostoyevsky
To the Lighthouse; Mrs Dalloway	Virginia Woolf
The Sorrows of Young Werther	Johann W. Goethe
Leaves of Grass - 1855 edition	Walt Whitman
Analects	Confucius
Beowulf	Anonymous
Plain Tales From The Hills	Rudyard Kipling
The Subjection of Women	John Stuart Mill
The Rights of Man	Thomas Paine
Progress and Poverty	Henry George
Captain Blood	Rafael Sabatini
Captains Courageous	Rudyard Kipling
The Meditations of Marcus Aurelius	Marcus Aurelius
The Social Contract	Jean Jacques Rousseau
War is a Racket	Smedley D. Butler
The Dead	James Joyce
The Old Wives' Tale	Arnold Bennett
Letters Concerning the English Nation	Voltaire
Portrait of the Artist As a Young Man	James Joyce
Coningsby	Benjamin Disraeli
Uncle Tom's Cabin	Harriet Beecher Stowe

Obtainable at all good online and local bookstores.
View Aziloth Books' full list at: www.azilothbooks.com

AZILOTH BOOKS | CHILDREN'S Classics

Aziloth Books is passionate about bringing the very best in children's classics fiction to the next generation of book-lovers. We believe in the transforming power of children's books to encourage a life-long love of reading, and publish only the best authors and illustrators. With its original design and outstanding quality, our highly successful list has something to suit every age and interest. Titles include:

The Railway Children	Edith Nesbit
Anne of Green Gables	Lucy Maud Montgomery
What Katy Did	Susan Coolidge
Puck of Pook's Hill	Rudyard Kipling
The Jungle Books	Rudyard Kipling
Just So Stories	Rudyard Kipling
Alice Through the Looking Glass	Charles Dodgson
Alice's Adventures in Wonderland*	Charles Dodgson
Black Beauty	Anna Sewell
The War of the Worlds	H. G Wells
The Time Machine	H. G .Wells
The Sleeper Awakes	H. G. Wells
The Invisible Man	H. G. Wells
The Lost World	Sir Arthur Conan Doyle
Gulliver's Travels*	Jonathan Swift
Catriona (David Balfour)	Robert Louis Stevenson
The Water Babies	Charles Kingsley
The First Men in the Moon	Jules Verne
The Secret Garden	Frances Hodgson Burnett
A Little Princess	Frances Hodgson Burnett
Peter Pan*	J. M. Barrie
The Song of Hiawatha*	Henry W. Longfellow
Tales from Shakespeare	Charles and Mary Lamb
The Wonderful Wizard of Oz	L. Frank Baum
The Complete Grimm's Fairy Tales	Jacob & Wilhelm Grimm

*with colour illustrations

Obtainable at all good online and local bookstores.
View Aziloth Books' full list at: www.azilothbooks.com